An Analysis of

Jay MacLeod's

Ain't No Makin' It

Aspirations and Attainment in a Low-Income Neighborhood

Anna Seiferle-Valencia

Published by Macat International Ltd
24:13 Coda Centre, 189 Munster Road, London SW6 6AW.

Distributed exclusively by Routledge
2 Park Square, Milton Park, Abingdon, Oxon OX14 4RN
711 Third Avenue, New York, NY 10017, USA

Routledge is an imprint of the Taylor & Francis Group, an informa business

www.macat.com
info@macat.com

Cataloguing in Publication Data
A catalogue record for this book is available from the British Library.
Library of Congress Cataloguing-in-Publication Data is available upon request.
Cover illustration: Etienne Gilfillan

ISBN 978-1-912302-10-9 (hardback)
ISBN 978-1-912128-74-7 (paperback)
ISBN 978-1-912128-35-8 (e-book)

CONTENTS

THE MACAT LIBRARY

The Macat Library is a series of unique academic explorations of seminal works in the humanities and social sciences – books and papers that have had a significant and widely recognised impact on their disciplines. It has been created to serve as much more than just a summary of what lies between the covers of a great book. It illuminates and explores the influences on, ideas of, and impact of that book. Our goal is to offer a learning resource that encourages critical thinking and fosters a better, deeper understanding of important ideas.

Each publication is divided into three Sections: Influences, Ideas, and Impact. Each Section has four Modules. These explore every important facet of the work, and the responses to it.

This Section-Module structure makes a Macat Library book easy to use, but it has another important feature. Because each Macat book is written to the same format, it is possible (and encouraged!) to cross-reference multiple Macat books along the same lines of inquiry or research. This allows the reader to open up interesting interdisciplinary pathways.

To further aid your reading, lists of glossary terms and people mentioned are included at the end of this book (these are indicated by an asterisk [*] throughout) – as well as a list of works cited.

Macat has worked with the University of Cambridge to identify the elements of critical thinking and understand the ways in which six different skills combine to enable effective thinking.
Three allow us to fully understand a problem; three more give us the tools to solve it. Together, these six skills make up the **PACIER** model of critical thinking. They are:

ANALYSIS – understanding how an argument is built
EVALUATION – exploring the strengths and weaknesses of an argument
INTERPRETATION – understanding issues of meaning

CREATIVE THINKING – coming up with new ideas and fresh connections
PROBLEM-SOLVING – producing strong solutions
REASONING – creating strong arguments

To find out more, visit **WWW.MACAT.COM.**

CRITICAL THINKING AND *AIN'T NO MAKIN' IT*

Primary critical thinking skill: PROBLEM-SOLVING
Secondary critical thinking skill: REASONING

Why is it that children from disadvantaged backgrounds find it so difficult – and often impossible – to achieve? Few questions are of such fundamental importance to the functioning of a fair and effective society than this one, yet the academic and political narratives that exist to explain the problem are fundamentally contradictory: some say the root of the problem lies in racial prejudice; others that the key factor is class; others again argue that we should look first at laziness, government's commitment to provide demotivating 'safety nets,' and to the appeal of easy money earned from a criminal lifestyle. Jay Macleod's seminal work of anthropology is one of the most influential studies to address this issue, and – in suggesting that problems of class, above all, help to fuel continued social inequality, Macleod is engaging in an important piece of problem-solving. He asks the right questions, basing his study on two different working class subcultures, one white and largely devoid of aspiration and the other black and much more ambitious and conformist. By showing that the members of both groups find it equally hard to achieve their dreams – that there really 'Ain't no makin' it,' as his title proposes – Macleod issues a direct challenge to the ideology of the American Dream, and by extension to the social contract that underpinned American society and politics for the duration of the twentieth century. His work – robustly structured and well-reasoned – is now frequently studied in universities, and it offers a sharp corrective to those who insist that the poor could control their own destinies if they choose to do so.

ABOUT THE AUTHOR OF THE ORIGINAL WORK

Born in 1961, American sociologist **Jay MacLeod** grew up in New Hampshire. He studied sociology at Harvard University and turned his senior honors thesis examining the impact of poverty on the lives of young Americans into a 1987 book, *Ain't No Makin' It*. In 1991 he published a work about the civil rights movement—*Minds Stayed on Freedom*—and moved to England to become a parish priest in the Anglican Church. Despite pursuing a career outside academia, MacLeod continued to update *Ain't No Makin' It*. He returned to the US in 2013 to take up a position as rector in a church in New Hampshire.

ABOUT THE AUTHOR OF THE ANALYSIS

Dr Anna Seiferle-Valencia holds a PhD in anthropology from Harvard. She was formerly curator of Latin American Art at the Tuscon Museum of Art, Arizona.

ABOUT MACAT

GREAT WORKS FOR CRITICAL THINKING

Macat is focused on making the ideas of the world's great thinkers accessible and comprehensible to everybody, everywhere, in ways that promote the development of enhanced critical thinking skills.

It works with leading academics from the world's top universities to produce new analyses that focus on the ideas and the impact of the most influential works ever written across a wide variety of academic disciplines. Each of the works that sit at the heart of its growing library is an enduring example of great thinking. But by setting them in context – and looking at the influences that shaped their authors, as well as the responses they provoked – Macat encourages readers to look at these classics and game-changers with fresh eyes. Readers learn to think, engage and challenge their ideas, rather than simply accepting them.

'Macat offers an amazing first-of-its-kind tool for interdisciplinary learning and research. Its focus on works that transformed their disciplines and its rigorous approach, drawing on the world's leading experts and educational institutions, opens up a world-class education to anyone.'

Andreas Schleicher
Director for Education and Skills, Organisation for Economic Co-operation and Development

'Macat is taking on some of the major challenges in university education ... They have drawn together a strong team of active academics who are producing teaching materials that are novel in the breadth of their approach.'

Prof Lord Broers,
former Vice-Chancellor of the University of Cambridge

'The Macat vision is exceptionally exciting. It focuses upon new modes of learning which analyse and explain seminal texts which have profoundly influenced world thinking and so social and economic development. It promotes the kind of critical thinking which is essential for any society and economy.
This is the learning of the future.'

Rt Hon Charles Clarke, former UK Secretary of State for Education

'The Macat analyses provide immediate access to the critical conversation surrounding the books that have shaped their respective discipline, which will make them an invaluable resource to all of those, students and teachers, working in the field.'

Professor William Tronzo, University of California at San Diego

WAYS IN TO THE TEXT

KEY POINTS

- Jay MacLeod is a Harvard-educated sociologist,* social activist, and ordained Anglican* priest.
- Published in 1987, *Ain't No Makin' It* argues that families remain in poverty from one generation to the next in American society because of structural inequality.* For example, schools tend to treat poor students in ways that keep them poor. Poverty is not the result of personal failures or shortcomings.
- The book challenges assumptions about the causes of poverty and why it continues. MacLeod looks at how social structures* (the social networks through which individuals interact), the economy, personal choice, racism,* and available opportunities impact success over an individual's lifetime.

Who Is Jay MacLeod?

US sociologist John M. "Jay" MacLeod was born in 1961 and grew up in rural New Hampshire, the son of white lower-middle-class parents. He graduated from high school in 1979 and enrolled at Harvard University,* where he undertook sociological research in Boston as part of his senior honors thesis. MacLeod went on to publish that research as *Ain't No Makin' It: Leveled Aspirations in a*

Low-Income Neighborhood in 1987. (Future editions of the text were titled *Ain't No Makin' It: Aspirations and Attainment in a Low-Income Neighborhood.)* The 1980s were a period of extreme social inequality* in the United States and MacLeod made a major contribution to our understanding of that period.

After completing his degree, he studied at Oxford University* in Great Britain, thanks to a Rhodes scholarship,* one of the most prestigious one-year scholarships in the world. Afterward he returned to the United States to work as a community organizer* in rural Mississippi.

While working in Mississippi, MacLeod applied what he had learned writing *Ain't No Makin' It* in his work with local youth. MacLeod's students interviewed veterans of the Civil Rights Movement,* and he then analyzed the results of their study using many of the same approaches he had used in *Ain't No Makin' It.*

In 1991, MacLeod moved to England to serve as a parish priest in the Anglican Church. Despite pursuing a career outside academia, he continued with his sociological research. He returned to the United States later that year and again in 2006 to interview the Hallway Hangers and the Brothers, the two groups of young men he had written about in *Ain't No Makin' It.* These follow-up interviews helped provide an insight into how the youthful experiences of these young men continued to impact them as adults.

Although his writings have attracted plenty of interest from scholars and show a deep commitment to social justice* throughout the research project, MacLeod's publications are aimed at a general audience.

What Does *Ain't No Makin' It* Say?

In *Ain't No Makin' It,* Jay MacLeod argues that poverty is the result of the structure of American society itself, rather than laziness, lack of willpower, or personal moral failure on the part of individuals. He supports this point with both sociological theory and interviews conducted with two groups of urban youths living in the same public housing* development. MacLeod began interviewing the young men when they were still in high school and aged between 14 and 18.

During the next two decades after the publication of *Ain't No Makin' It* he followed the same groups of men to show how a youth spent in poverty impacts a man throughout his entire adult life.

In *Ain't No Makin' It* MacLeod investigates the role that belief in the American Dream* plays in guiding the hopes of these two groups of young men. One group, mostly white, does not have faith in the American Dream and feels that lifetime opportunities are limited. Known as the Hallway Hangers, they have low ambitions, drink, smoke, use and sell drugs, are prone to violence, and express racist viewpoints. Status in the group depends on physical strength and the ability to fight. The other group, the Brothers, is mostly black. They *do* believe in the American Dream, have higher ambitions, abide by the law, avoid drugs and alcohol, attend school, and work hard to get ahead in life.

MacLeod's study reveals the factors that influence how these young men see their life prospects. He focuses on the social inequality that results from class* differences as a driving factor in the lifetime success (or otherwise) of these men. Despite their different youthful views of the American Dream, very few of the men in either group go on to achieve the middle-class* lifestyle they aspired to as teenagers. MacLeod's work asks why teenagers who do well in school, avoid drugs and crime, have supportive parents, and believe in the American Dream still cannot succeed despite their best efforts.

Now viewed as a classic by sociologists and often assigned as a text in sociology courses, MacLeod's study challenges widely held ideas about race, violence, and poverty in the United States. It shows that the idea of the American Dream does not equate with the realities of inequality based on socioeconomic* class in the United States. Simply stated, the study asserts that capitalist* societies tend to produce structural inequalities. This means that the structures of a capitalist society, such as its schools, often limit achievement. People will inevitably discover that their hopes and dreams are limited by the social conditions they find themselves in. MacLeod argues that the American Dream—the idea that with sufficient hard work, anyone can be economically successful—only helps to hide the reality of social inequality in the United States.

Ain't No Makin' It is still relevant today because inequality still exists in American society and in many other societies around the world. A lack of personal financial success is often attributed to an individual's shortcomings. But MacLeod's study shows that working hard and believing in the ideal of equal opportunity does not guarantee success. Instead, success is a complex interaction between individuals, social structure, class, inequality, racism, and cultural viewpoints. This does not mean that young people from poor neighborhoods cannot achieve a middle-class life—or even become well-off. Some do. But the hurdles placed in their path are much greater than they are for young people from more privileged backgrounds. As a result, far fewer poor children manage to break into the middle-class lifestyle.

MacLeod's study helps clarify the root causes of unequal access to opportunity and shows how we can create more just societies. Scholars and communities alike continue to build on MacLeod's approaches as they try to develop solutions for addressing social inequality.

Why Does *Ain't No Makin' It* Matter?

Ain't No Makin' It helps us understand the causes of social inequality, especially in capitalist societies. If economic success is available to everybody in society, then why do some become increasingly rich while others remain poor? Why do we not observe more upward mobility?

Many Americans believe that laziness, drug addiction, and individual character failings cause people to live in poverty and to be homeless, and they are not aware of the degree to which social structures, such as schools, workplaces, and the justice system, create conditions of inequality. MacLeod shows that the urban poor do their best to create meaning and value in their lives despite severely limiting social circumstances. In reality, it is social and economic structures themselves that continually recreate inequality and poverty (that is, social reproduction).* So the only way to solve these problems is to alter the social conditions that produce inequality in the first place.

It is not down to differences in race, intelligence, or character. Within the United States, people tend not to escape their social class from one generation to the next despite the generally accepted view that American society is open and full of opportunity for people to move upwards. The gap between the rich and the poor is much greater in the United States than in many other developed countries. But in many places around the world, the poor are blamed for their own conditions, which often has negative political, economic, and policy consequences for the poor themselves. *Ain't No Makin' It* makes it clear that in order to create more just societies, we must first create more just social structures.

MacLeod's balanced study shows how methods from anthropology* and sociology can be combined to help us understand complex social problems, bringing together the anthropological focus on individual experience with a sociological analysis of social structures like schools. It also appeals to those interested in economics as it provides detailed examples of how economic systems affect individuals. In short, anybody who is interested in the relationship between an individual and his/her culture should read *Ain't No Makin' It.*

SECTION 1
INFLUENCES

MODULE 1
THE AUTHOR AND THE HISTORICAL CONTEXT

KEY POINTS

- *Ain't No Makin' It* makes use of extensive interviews with two groups of boys of high-school age to examine how America's class* structure influences people to stay in poverty from generation to generation.
- MacLeod first published *Ain't No Makin' It* in 1987 after finishing college and while working as a community organizer* promoting civil rights* in Mississippi.
- The 1980s was a period of highly unequal distribution of wealth* (the manner in which wealth is proportionately shared out through a society), with drastic governmental cuts to public social programs, increased youth crime, and record levels of homelessness.

Why Read This Text?

Jay MacLeod's *Ain't No Makin' It* shines a light on the inner workings of the cycles of poverty and social inequality*—the unequal distribution of resources and opportunities within a society along the lines of social class—in the United States. MacLeod interviewed two groups of young men from a public housing project* in the Boston area that he chose to call Clarendon Heights in order to protect those he interviewed. This was for a thesis he was writing while studying sociology* at university.

MacLeod returned to interview the same people over the next 24 years, and these follow-up interviews were included in the second and third editions of the text. In the book, MacLeod analyzes how the

> **"I might have been closer in class background to the people of Clarendon Heights than the great bulk of my university classmates were, but neither my lower-middle-class origins nor my attendance at a regional high school in New Hampshire made me particularly 'at home' in the [housing] project. Most important, I was a university student, a status that could breed resentment, for it implied an upward social trajectory to which these people do not have ready access."**
>
> Jay MacLeod, *Ain't No Makin' It: Aspirations and Attainment in a Low-Income Neighborhood*

dynamics behind poverty are reproduced from one generation to the next and how this is the result of a complex interaction of personal decisions, cultural attitudes, hopes and aspirations,* and the constraints of a capitalist* economy and society.

MacLeod uses the methods of ethnography* (the study of different cultures) by interviewing members of two groups of boys to compare their experiences and identify how poverty is maintained in both groups. One group, the "Hallway Hangers," is mostly white, and many in the group have already dropped out of high school. The other group is the mostly black "Brothers," all of whom are still in school. MacLeod's work uncovers the fact that the structure of modern American society offers nothing like an equal playing field, and "confirms that structural inequality* causes poverty. The presumed behavioral and cultural deficiencies of the lower class are the consequence rather than the cause of poverty."[1] For example, members of the urban poor sell drugs because their social circumstances severely limit their access to stable jobs. While selling drugs is illegal, it provides an income that is otherwise hard to come by when living in conditions of social poverty. This is an important consideration today, as America and other societies around the world debate policy decisions that directly impact equal access to education, health care, and jobs that pay a living wage (that is, a wage paying enough to provide a reasonable standard of living).

Ain't No Makin' It also examines how valid the ideas of equality and upward mobility*—ideologies* that form a key part of America's identity—really are. More broadly the book examines capitalist economies in general. In many cases, Americans make failure personal, blaming people's individual shortcomings if they have not succeeded in life. MacLeod's insightful analysis shows how the structure of American society creates the conditions for failure by limiting the opportunities for individuals born into a low-class structure to achieve. In doing so, MacLeod exposes the structures and dynamics of the American class system that ensure poverty passes from generation to generation.

Author's Life

John M. "Jay" MacLeod is an American sociologist and currently a parish priest. He is originally from a lower-middle-class background in rural New Hampshire[2] and graduated from high school in 1979 before enrolling at the prestigious Harvard University,* where he studied sociology. The first publication of *Ain't No Makin' It* in 1987 grew out of MacLeod's senior honors thesis in 1984. MacLeod won a prestigious Rhodes scholarship* to spend a year at Oxford University* in England before spending four years in Holmes County, Mississippi working as a community organizer.

In 1991 he published *Minds Stayed on Freedom,* a book that told the story of the struggle for civil rights in rural Mississippi from the perspective of veterans of the Civil Rights Movement who were interviewed by local youths. That same year MacLeod left the US for England, where he studied theology at Lincoln Theological College.* By the end of the updated *Ain't No Makin' It,* the reader learns that

MacLeod has begun serving an ethnically diverse community in Lincoln, England as a parish priest. He discusses his religious calling with curious members of the Hallway Hangers and the Brothers when he returns for follow-up interviews.

At the end of the book MacLeod includes an appendix, featuring information about his interview methods and personal experiences."I hope this book does justice to the young lives of the Brothers and the Hallway Hangers. I hope it ... provokes further study and sparks a critical attitude toward the American socioeconomic* system. Most of all, I hope it spurs readers to struggle for a society that doesn't trample on the aspirations of its people."[3] Throughout his academic and professional career, Jay MacLeod has consistently demonstrated his commitment to social justice.*

Author's Background

MacLeod published *Ain't No Makin' It* in 1987. At that time Ronald Reagan* was in his second term as US president, having been sworn in to office in 1981. Many of Reagan's policies were believed to have had wide-ranging negative impacts on the poor, especially the urban poor such as the residents of "Clarendon Heights." By the end of Reagan's second term, federal assistance to local governments had been cut by 60 percent and federal aid comprised only 6 percent of big-city budgets. As a result, a number of police and fire departments, sanitation departments, municipal hospitals and health clinics, subsidized housing projects, schools and public libraries were closed in poor urban areas.[4] At the same time, urban homelessness was at an all-time high. Violent crime increased dramatically in the early 1980s and again in the early 1990s, largely due to increasing youth crime.[5] The rich in America became richer during Reagan's administration and the gap between the rich and poor grew.[6] Many people failed to see a connection between social inequalities and the cutting of services on the one hand, and increases in crime and homelessness on the other.

Instead they argued that homelessness and poverty were somehow the result of people's own (often moral) failings.

MacLeod could not have picked a better time to publish his study of poor young urban men. By choosing to focus on one black group and one white group, MacLeod also challenged popular preconceptions that the urban poor were predominantly black and that black youths were responsible for most violent crime. MacLeod's work can clearly be seen as politically engaged, and as he expanded his text for subsequent editions of *Ain't No Makin' It*, he came out even more strongly in favor of reform in the educational system and class structure of the United States.

NOTES

1 Jay MacLeod, *Ain't No Makin' It: Aspirations and Attainment in a Low-Income Neighborhood* (Boulder, Colorado: Westview Press, 2009), 267.

2 MacLeod, *Ain't No Makin' It*, 487.

3 MacLeod, *Ain't No Makin' It*, 496.

4 Peter Dreier, "Reagan's Legacy: Homelessness in America," *National Housing Institute* 135 (2004), accessed September 30, 2015, http://www.nhi.org/online/issues/135/reagan.html.

5 Jeffrey A. Butts and Jeremy Travis, "The Rise and Fall of American Youth Violence: 1980 to 2000," *Urban Institute* 2002, accessed September 30, 2015, http://www.urban.org/research/publication/rise-and-fall-american-youth-violence/view/full_report.

6 Dreier, "Reagan's Legacy."

MODULE 2
ACADEMIC CONTEXT

KEY POINTS

- Sociology* is concerned with the study of the origins, development, causes, and structure of how humans behave in groups. *Ain't No Makin' It* focuses on the sociological question of how inequality is somehow passed from one generation to the next in American society.
- MacLeod uses theories of structuralism*, Marxism,* and other sociological schools of thought to explore social reproduction*—how schools and other institutions continually recreate society's class* structures.
- MacLeod focuses on the concept of social capital*—the value of social networks and personal connections from which an individual benefits— as he examines how individual aspirations* grow out of a marriage between personal desires and an understanding of the limits of one's social situation.

The Work in its Context

In *Ain't No Makin' It: Aspirations and Attainment in a Low-Income Neighborhood* Jay MacLeod uses a sociological approach to answer the question of why there is a strong tendency for children from the working classes* to end up working class themselves. This question interested sociologists for the better part of a century. Sociologists tend to focus on themes of social order, disorder, and change. MacLeod's study focuses on one particular question: how does poverty seem to recur from generation to generation in American society?

The 1980s in the United States was a period of unparalleled economic growth, but it was also a period when the gap between rich

> **“The idea of potential equality of power has been ... fitted to a competitive society where *in*equality of power is the rule and expectation. If all men start on some basis of equal potential ability, then the inequalities they experience in their lives ... are the logical consequences of different personal drives ... in other words, social differences can now appear as questions of character, of moral resolve, will, and competence.”**
>
> Richard Sennett and Jonathan Cobb, *The Hidden Injuries of Class*

and poor increased. Homelessness and violent crime also rose dramatically. The urban poor came under closer scrutiny from politicians, law enforcement agencies, government agencies, and scholars. Were the urban poor *really* more violent than suburban* Americans? Was a lack of education the problem? Would vocational training* in high schools—education that prepares students for jobs in a particular field—solve these problems?

As an undergraduate student at the prestigious Harvard University* in the early 1980s, Jay MacLeod enjoyed the resources of the nation's largest, most reputable, and wealthiest university. Across the Charles River, meanwhile, Boston's poor urban neighborhoods remained some of the most economically depressed in the nation. MacLeod's research work for *Ain't No Makin' It* reflects the broader questions circulating in American society at the time. He challenges conventional thought by turning many accepted ideas about race, poverty, and class on their heads and does so by analyzing interviews with poor urban youth within a broader sociological theory. This method helps the reader make connections between the individual stories MacLeod is telling and his broader points.

Overview of the Field

MacLeod's approach is dialectical* (that is, concerned with the relationships between social, cultural, and economic factors), and so he focuses on the desires of the two groups of youths he studies—the Hallway Hangers and the Brothers—and their limited social, economic, and educational circumstances. In order to do this he evaluates the impact that social structures* such as the economy, the educational system, and family environment have on the two groups.

MacLeod's work was influenced by major thinkers in sociology from the past 150 years. The theory of structuralism was one approach that helped him develop his ideas. Structuralism originated in the early 1900s when Swiss language specialist Ferdinand de Saussure* argued that languages could be understood by studying not just the individual parts of speech, but the relationships between them. De Saussure's approach to linguistics (the scientific study of the form, meaning, and sociocultural context of language) spread to other fields, such as sociology and economics.* In the field of sociology, structuralism focuses on the function of individual parts of a society.

In the 1950s the sociologist Talcott Parsons* built on de Saussure's ideas to develop a structural-functionalist* approach.[1] Structural-functionalism focuses on society as a complex system of related parts that function together. For Parsons, society is reproduced as individuals get used to what is considered culturally normal and are exposed to the consequences of not following these norms—embarrassment, shaming, fines, imprisonment, etc.[2] Robert K. Merton* developed Parsons's theory by recognizing that a social structure can have a number of functions. For example, a school educates children in academic subjects, but also prepares students to fill a role in society based on their social class. Merton also argues that society limits individual agency*—the ability of individual people to act—and that when faced with these limits, individuals react in a number of ways. They conform, participate without expecting a positive outcome, withdraw, innovate (that is, they think up new ways to respond), or they rebel.[3] The young men MacLeod interviews show a number of these reactions.

MacLeod's study also relies on the concept of social reproduction, a central idea of the economic model identified by Karl Marx.* Marx was a nineteenth- century sociologist, economist, and philosopher best known for his negative views of modern capitalism.* For Marx, society reproduces itself and maintains the same features, generation after generation, via its social and economic structures. In a capitalist society, this means that the hierarchy of workers in the labor system* (that is, the different categories of workers, defined according to their pay and their privileges) are recreated from one generation to the next. MacLeod investigates how this same idea of social reproduction can be applied to the aspirations and then the actual achievements of urban male youth.

Academic Influences

The idea that how people's lives turn out is determined by the structures of the society they live in can be called deterministic.* A deterministic model suggesting that society reproduces itself with each new generation argues that the capitalist economy creates roles for individuals based on their social class, and does not allow them much say in deciding what their role in life will be. MacLeod identifies the theories of twentieth-century economists Samuel Bowles* and Herbert Gintis* as offering such a model. According to these thinkers, the institution of the school is responsible for reproducing social classes. "Schools train the wealthy to take up places at the top of the economy while conditioning the poor to accept their lowly status in the class structure."[4] MacLeod builds on this idea in his investigation of the role the local high school (which is state-funded) plays in the lives of the people he follows, specifically arguing that the structure of the school lowers the aspirations of his informants* (the anthropological* term for people who give anthropologists information in the field). He believes this is especially true for the most marginalized students.

MacLeod also relies extensively on the theories of the French sociologist and anthropologist Pierre Bourdieu,* especially what Bourdieu refers to as cultural capital* and habitus,* which broadly mean the shared views of members of the same group or class. Bourdieu focused his research on power dynamics within societies. He argued that there are four kinds of capital contributing to social reproduction: economic capital* (resources that can be measured in money), cultural capital (for example, a person's physical appearance and accent), social capital* (the value of social networks and personal connections from which people can benefit), and human capital* (the knowledge and personal attributes a person can apply towards their work to be financially successful). Cultural capital, or general cultural background knowledge, is "the centerpiece of Bourdieu's theory of cultural reproduction,"[5] and MacLeod applies the idea extensively in his own study, especially when looking at the job market.

MacLeod incorporates Bourdieu's definition of the habitus, a "subjective but not individual system of internalized [ways of looking at the world] common to all members of the same group or class."[6] The aspirations held by an individual may feel very personal, but Bourdieu and MacLeod argue that "aspirations are not the product of rational analysis; rather, they are acquired in the habitus of the individual."[7] In other words, individuals form their ambitions based on the norms they see around them. The aspiration of a child from a rich family may be to become a financier or business owner. For a child from a lower-class family, it may be to get a factory job. Following Bourdieu, MacLeod argues that individual aspiration is actually a compromise between personal desires and an understanding of the limits of social circumstance.

NOTES

1 Talcott Parsons and Edward A. Shils, *Toward a General Theory of Action* (Cambridge: Harvard University Press, 1976), 190.

2 Talcott Parsons et al., *Theories of Society: Foundations of Modern Sociological Theory* (New York: Free Press, 1961).

3 Robert K. Merton, *Social Theory and Social Structure* (New York: Free Press, 1968).

4 Jay MacLeod, *Ain't No Makin' It: Aspirations and Attainment in a Low-Income Neighborhood* (Boulder, Colorado: Westview Press, 2009), 12.

5 MacLeod, *Ain't No Makin' It*, 13.

6 Pierre Bourdieu, *Outline of a Theory of Practice* (Cambridge: Cambridge University Press, 1977), 82–3.

7 MacLeod, *Ain't No Makin' It*, 15.

MODULE 3
THE PROBLEM

KEY POINTS

- **In *Ain't No Makin' It*, Jay MacLeod looks at the combination of socioeconomic* structure and personal choice to explore how poverty is "passed on" from one generation to the next.**
- **The book was published in 1987, at a time when popular and political opinion claimed that the urban poor were responsible for their situation, often because of their own moral shortcomings.**
- **MacLeod challenged popular assumptions about the causes of poverty and social inequality* in the United States, rejecting simplistic notions that poverty was the result of race or some kind of personal failure.**

Core Question

In *Ain't No Makin' It,* Jay MacLeod sets out to answer why poverty is transmitted from one generation to the next in American society. This research question reflects not only academic concerns, but also broader popular concerns that people in American society and politics had in the 1980s. At that time, the unequal distribution of wealth* in the United States was reaching a new peak, with the top 1 percent of the population owning 37 percent of national wealth, and the top 10 percent owning 86 percent of it.[1] The gap between rich and poor has, in fact, grown even bigger since then. By the end of President Reagan's second term in 1989, 32 million Americans were living below the poverty line*[2] and federal assistance to local governments for public services, such as employment centers, legal services and public transport, had been slashed.[3] The result of these policies was to further disadvantage the urban poor, who were already struggling.

> **“The chapters that follow examine in an intensive fashion two very different groups from the same social location and in the process illuminate some of the mechanisms, both structural and cultural, that contribute to social reproduction. In particular, occupational aspirations, as a mediating link between socioeconomic structures (what society offers) and individuals at the cultural level (what one wants), play a crucial role in the reproduction of class inequality.”**
>
> Jay MacLeod, *Ain't No Makin' It: Aspirations and Attainment in a Low-Income Neighborhood*

MacLeod's study is important in the context of the early 1980s because he investigated not just the social consequences of poverty, but how social inequality is passed on. Furthermore, he focuses on poor urban white youth *and* poor urban black youth, challenging the simplistic idea that poverty is a racial problem. He argues that the cause of the transmission of poverty must come from the relationship between two things: the structure of the socioeconomic system and the choices available to individuals. In doing so, MacLeod rejects the possibility that poverty and social inequality is the result of laziness, poor personal choice, violent tendencies, or moral failure. By designing his study as he does, MacLeod makes sure he reveals the humanity of his participants. He also shows how their decisions reflect their understanding of the opportunities that are available to them.

The Participants

The primary challenge MacLeod addresses in *Ain't No Makin' It* is how to take a varied body of data and use it to produce a clear explanation of the relationship between individual experience and social structure.* He integrates various sociological* theories in his interpretation of the information he collects in interviews. His argument is not directed against any particular school of thought, but can be thought of as a challenge to society in general and the reader in particular to think about, and improve, the state of social inequality in the United States.

Issues of poverty and homelessness were topics of national debate and discussion in the United States in the 1980s when MacLeod began his study. Social scientists were working to understand the social and cultural dynamics that were passing poverty from one generation to the next. During his time as US president, Ronald Reagan* tried to remove federal housing assistance to the poor, while making cuts to federal programs. Public housing projects* like "Clarendon Heights"—a real place with a fictitious name—where MacLeod conducted his study, depended on federal aid. Cuts to housing subsidies were accompanied by a rise in homelessness, with an estimated 600,000 people homeless in the US on any given night in the late 1980s.[4] This number included many children, war veterans, and workers who had recently been laid off. The urban poor were openly criticized for their own conditions, with the president stating on national television that homelessness was a choice[5] and using exaggerated stories of a "welfare* queen" (a deprecatory phrase mainly used to describe women who collect excessive welfare payments) in Chicago to justify cuts in federal support.[6] These comments reflected a commonly held public opinion about the relationship between poverty and success, and seemed to confirm the idea that poor people remained poor by choice, through laziness, or through their own personal moral shortcomings.

The Contemporary Debate

In conducting his field research, MacLeod appears to have been significantly influenced by the work of earlier scholars such as Paul Willis.* Willis published *Learning to Labor* in 1977, roughly 10 years before MacLeod published *Ain't No Makin' It.* MacLeod describes Willis's work as an "impressive ethnographic* study of a group of disaffected, white working-class* males in a British secondary school."[7] Willis found that this group of boys had shared values that ran counter to mainstream* (beliefs or behaviors considered to be normal) British society. Willis was also writing in the Marxist* tradition, and argued that the boys' decisions were influenced by their class* background, geographical location, local job market, and their educational success or failure.

MacLeod follows a similar approach in studying the two groups of youths from Clarendon Heights—the Hallway Hangers and the Brothers. Like Willis, he identifies the same range of factors as potential influences on the boys. Unlike Willis, however, MacLeod focuses on two contrasting groups: the group that develops its own set of counterculture* values—the Hallway Hangers—and the group that follows more traditional values and social expectations—the Brothers. He does this to compare and contrast how the same socioeconomic setting can influence people in different ways. MacLeod further argues that poverty is a *class* issue, not a race issue: "By bringing the white poor into view, our story dissolves the mistaken connection between African Americans and behavior associated with poverty—crime, family disruption, substance abuse, and so on."[8] In fact, MacLeod finds that drug use, alcoholism, truancy, and crime are associated with the white Hallway Hangers. The African American Brothers, on the other hand, are responsible, attend school, and avoid alcohol and drugs. Yet the results of the study are striking because they reveal how every single young man is disadvantaged by the same limitations, regardless of how he perceives his possibilities, or even the efforts he makes to escape his circumstances and attain the American Dream.*

NOTES

1 Cornel West, *Race Matters* (Boston: Beacon Press, 1993), 6.

2 Manning Marable, *Race, Reform, and Rebellion: The Second Reconstruction in Black America 1945–1990* (Jackson: University Press of Mississippi, 1991), 207.

3 Peter Dreier, "Reagan's Legacy: Homelessness in America," *National Housing Institute* 135 (2004), accessed September 30, 2015, http://www.nhi.org/online/issues/135/reagan.html.

4 Dreier, "Reagan's Legacy."

5 Steven V. Roberts, "Reagan on Homelessness: Many Choose to Live in the Streets," *New York Times,* December 23, 1988, accessed November 18, 2015, http://www.nytimes.com/1988/12/23/us/reagan-on-homelessness-many-choose-to-live-in-the-streets.html.

6 Gene Demby, "The Truth Behind the Lies of the Original 'Welfare Queen,'" *National Public Radio,* December 20, 2013, accessed November 18, 2015, http://www.npr.org/sections/codeswitch/2013/12/20/255819681/the-truth-behind-the-lies-of-the-original-welfare-queen.

7 Jay MacLeod, *Ain't No Makin' It: Aspirations and Attainment in a Low-Income Neighborhood* (Boulder, Colorado: Westview Press, 2009), 18.

8 MacLeod, *Ain't No Makin' It,* 243.

MODULE 4
THE AUTHOR'S CONTRIBUTION

KEY POINTS

- The central argument in *Ain't No Makin' It* is that social inequality* is ultimately the result of the structure of the American capitalist* economy, not because of personal failure on the behalf of individuals.
- MacLeod examines the ideology* (a system of beliefs or understandings) of the "American Dream,"* namely that through hard work, anyone can become economically successful.
- MacLeod's research goes beyond similar studies of poor young urban men by showing that class,* and not race, is the most important influence on the aspirations* of young men from working-class* families.

Author's Aims

In *Ain't No Makin' It,* Jay MacLeod sets out to answer a seemingly simple question. Why is it that children from working-class backgrounds tend to have working-class jobs in adulthood? How can this be, despite the fact that the United States is a society in which upward social mobility* is clearly possible? In answering these questions, MacLeod is looking to shine a light on the inner workings of social class, and how it is maintained from generation to generation.

MacLeod answers these questions through interviews he conducts with 15 teenage boys (his informants)* from a public housing project* he decided to call "Clarendon Heights." He then combines these interviews with sociological* theory; that is, studying the origins, causes, developments, and structure of group behavior. When viewed through the context of broader theory, the boys' interviews can be seen as

> "My analysis of the aspirations of the Brothers and Hallway Hangers shows clearly the autonomy individuals possess in their response to this received structure of domination. How poor youths react to an objective situation that is weighed heavily against them depends on a number of mediating factors and ultimately is contingent [subject to chance] ... Thus, we see how structure can reach into human consciousness to encourage dispositions that ensure the reproduction of class inequality."
>
> Jay MacLeod, *Ain't No Makin' It: Aspirations and Attainment in a Low-Income Neighborhood*

personal, individual experiences reflecting broader social processes. MacLeod's study makes it clear how the particular experience of an individual is directly impacted by the social structures* of his society.

MacLeod's study was first completed as part of his undergraduate thesis in sociology. He did not continue his academic work in sociology, but did return to interview his informants on two occasions over a period of more than 20 years. With each return visit, MacLeod recontextualized* and updated his original findings using the later interviews, but did not substantially revise his theoretical approach or interpretation. MacLeod's ability to situate individual experience within broader social phenomena, and his long-term dedication to the research project, raised some interesting questions and produced a convincing piece of work.

Approach

MacLeod puts together a theory that tries to combine personal choice and structural inequality* as an explanation for why social inequality is reproduced from generation to generation. This is an original way of thinking that helps clarify how people's aspirations* are, in fact, a compromise between what an individual wants to achieve in life, and his or her awareness (or indeed lack of awareness) of the limitations imposed on him by socioeconomic* circumstances.

MacLeod's use of people's aspirations to understand the relationship between individual choices and social structure is backed by his use of the theory of achievement ideology* in his analysis. Achievement ideology is a sociological theory that explains why many Americans believe that hard work leads to economic success. The well-known rags-to-riches stories of great American entrepreneurs show the importance of achievement ideology in American thought. As long as Americans believe that working hard gives everybody an equal chance of success, then they will continue to participate in the social structures of American society.

However, MacLeod asks what happens when an individual or group realizes that opportunities are not truly equal after all. Realizing that there are limits as to what they can achieve economically, the Hallway Hangers have lower aspirations and form a counterculture* promoting values that are the opposite of those of mainstream middle-class* America. The black Brothers, on the other hand, believe they have the same chance of success as everybody else, and work hard to stay in school, obey the law, and avoid drugs to achieve it. Even though they are also negatively impacted by racism,* the Brothers' aspirations are higher than those of the Hallway Hangers, in no small part because they still believe in mainstream American achievement ideology.

Contribution in Context

MacLeod's text addresses many of the questions that were widely circulating in the 1980s. Trying to understand the causes and consequences of urban poverty had grabbed everybody's attention. MacLeod's contribution is original, because it draws attention to individuals whose lives were affected by both the limits and the expectations of the American economy, rather than simply lumping them all together as "the urban poor."

MacLeod's longitudinal* research (meaning a study that runs for a long period of time) spans 24 years as he follows the teenagers into adulthood and on towards middle age. His work is very similar to that of the British sociologist Paul Willis,* who produced a similar style of ethnographic* study on two groups of poor male youths in England, though over a much shorter time span. Comparing the two groups he studied, MacLeod traces how the aspirations held by the youths impacted their adult lives. MacLeod builds on the theories of Willis, French sociologist Pierre Bourdieu,* and the American economists Samuel Bowles* and Herbert Gintis,* to demonstrate how individual choice and agency* (that is, the ability to act according to one's choices) are influenced by the realities of social inequality.

MacLeod came to the conclusion that it is primarily class, and not race, that influences the aspirations of these young men. In the concluding chapter of the second part of his book, MacLeod directs his argument at the structure of American society: "Our society is *structured* to create poverty and extreme economic inequality. There are simply not enough good jobs to go around."[1] At the same time, however, MacLeod cautions that his analysis should not be applied in an all-encompassing way. Occasionally the child of a working-class family may well grow up to be affluent. "Factors like a neighborhood's … social ecology … produce complex patterns that defy quantification,"[2] he says. In other words, the urban poor are not an indistinguishable mass that can be spoken about in general terms. Like all social groups, they are made up of complex and unique individuals doing their best to navigate the opportunities and challenges that life has dealt them.

NOTES

1 Jay MacLeod, *Ain't No Makin' It: Aspirations and Attainment in a Low-Income Neighborhood* (Boulder, Colorado: Westview Press, 2009), 241.

2 MacLeod, *Ain't No Makin' it,* 250.

SECTION 2
IDEAS

MODULE 5
MAIN IDEAS

KEY POINTS

- **In *Ain't No Makin' It*, Jay MacLeod compares and contrasts the two groups of young men he follows. One group does not believe that working hard at school will gain them anything; the other has faith in the power of hard work.**
- **MacLeod argues that social classes* are maintained over time above all by individuals' occupational aspirations,* meaning the types of jobs they aim for.**
- **The book effectively has three parts. Part one is the original 1987 study; part two (1995) is based on interviews with the young men some years later; part three (2009) returns to the men, now in early middle age.**

Key Themes

In *Ain't No Makin' It,* Jay MacLeod addresses how class inequality* is reproduced from one generation to the next.All of the points he develops in the text can be tied to this central question. MacLeod attempts to answer it by studying the aspirations of two groups of young men, the Hallway Hangers (a majority white group) and the Brothers (a majority black group), all of whom live in a public housing project* in Boston.

In order to address how "poverty circumscribes [limits] the horizons of young people and how, at the societal level, the class structure is reproduced,"[1] MacLeod relies on a few key themes. The first is social reproduction,* a sociological theory that suggests how social relationships are maintained through time and over generations. Specifically, MacLeod puts forward the idea that occupational aspirations (the type of job a young person aims for), as a "mediating link between socioeconomic* structures (what society offers) and

> **"The picture that emerges from this ethnography deviates substantially from the myth of America as the land of opportunity in which any child can grow up to be president. American society is not as open as we like to think: the ladder of social mobility is not accessible to all, nor are its rungs easy to grasp ... For many of those in the lowest reaches of the social structure, the American Dream is a hallucination."**
>
> Jay MacLeod, *Ain't No Makin' It: Aspirations and Attainment in a Low-Income Neighborhood*

individuals at the cultural level (what one wants), play a crucial role in the reproduction of class inequality."[2] The importance of aspiration is highlighted throughout the text. However, MacLeod also identifies other factors that contribute to social reproduction, such as class-based differences in the way people speak, and where they were educated. He argues that "the regulation of aspiration is perhaps the most important"[3]—meaning that shaping the kind of work that young people aspire toward is the single most important factor in keeping them in the same social class as their parents.

The second major theme in the text is that of achievement ideology.* MacLeod examines aspiration under the lens of achievement ideology, or the socially constructed belief that working hard is the key to economic success. Though this ideology has long been at the core of the American Dream,* MacLeod illustrates the degree to which poor urban youth question whether the American Dream really does apply to them at all. MacLeod's study compares and contrasts the aspirations and the belief in achievement ideology in the two groups of young men he studies. His findings are in some cases paradoxical—seemingly absurd or contradictory—and often challenge the simplistic stereotypical picture of poor urban youth.

Exploring the Ideas

MacLeod focuses on two groups of teenage boys to evaluate the impact that aspirations have on lifetime success and the reproduction of social inequality.* The groups are strikingly different from each other, despite living in the same public housing complex. The Hallway Hangers are an almost entirely white group of young men who smoke, use and sell drugs, commit crimes, and have violent outbursts. When MacLeod began working with them, many identified themselves as alcoholics and all but two had already been arrested. The Hallway Hangers are proud of the status of being "bad," which MacLeod identifies as "being inextricably bound up with the premium put on masculinity, physical toughness, and street wisdom in lower-class culture."[4] Status for members in the group is primarily determined by their fighting ability.

The Brothers are a core group of seven high-school students who appear to be the complete opposite of the Hallway Hangers. The Brothers have only one white member. The Brothers all attend high school regularly and none of them smoke, drink regularly, or use drugs. None had been arrested when MacLeod began working with them. The differences in attitude of these two groups also extend to their aspirations about the kind of jobs they might be able to do, and their ability to achieve those aspirations over the course of their adult lives.

The Hallway Hangers reject the idea that hard work, especially in school, will lead to future success. They view their chances for upward mobility* as very remote and, as a result, they have low occupational aspirations.[5] This attitude is reinforced by their parents, who are reluctant to encourage their sons to have aspirations beyond what they feel can realistically be achieved.[6] The Brothers, on the other hand, believe that they *do* have opportunities to improve their economic situation, and that working hard will eventually be rewarded with the success of a steady, well-paying job. Because the Brothers believe in American achievement ideology more wholeheartedly, they have higher aspirations than the Hallway Hangers. Also, their aspirations are encouraged by their parents.[7] Even though they are subject to racism,* which the Hallway Hangers do not experience, the Brothers sense that there are fewer barriers to their success, even though, objectively, there are actually more. The Brothers believe that American society is fair and open based on their understanding of the civil rights* advances made by their parents' generation. The Hallway Hangers, however, believe their opportunities are limited and, as a result, turn to racism as a means of venting their frustration.

Language and Expression

The language in *Ain't No Makin' It* moves from the academic tone of MacLeod's sections on sociological theory to the vulgarities, racial slurs, and street slang as spoken by the members of the Hallway Hangers and the Brothers. Overall, the text is intended for an educated reader, but MacLeod is careful to explain jargon. His sociological theory is easy to follow because he structures his arguments clearly and uses accessible language. Readers who are less familiar with sociological terms and theory may want to use other reference sources, but only if they are looking for a deeper understanding. In most cases MacLeod provides enough explanation to make his point clear. For example, when explaining why individuals may be drawn to crime when faced with a difficult financial situation, MacLeod states that "the allure of a career in the underground economy makes sense only when measured against the option of an underpaid menial job."[8] MacLeod reinforces many of his ideas with this kind of straightforward language.

Ain't No Makin' It is organized into three parts. Part one is the original study published in 1987. Part two is a much-expanded second edition that was published in 1995 after MacLeod had first followed up with his informants. Here he interviews the Hallway Hangers and the Brothers in their twenties and analyzes his updated findings using the same model he opted for in part one. Part three of the text follows the informants towards middle age and was published in 2009. So the structure reflects a long-term study and allows the reader to follow both the lives of the participants *and* the development of MacLeod's interpretations of what he finds.

The text is structured as alternating sections, one being the more theoretical writings containing MacLeod's analysis of his data, and the other the interviews with the Hallway Hangers and the Brothers.

NOTES

1 Jay MacLeod, *Ain't No Makin' It: Aspirations and Attainment in a Low-Income Neighborhood* (Boulder, Colorado: Westview Press, 2009), 10.

2 MacLeod, *Ain't No Makin' It*, 22.

3 MacLeod, *Ain't No Makin' It*, 23.

4 MacLeod, *Ain't No Makin' It*, 28.

5 MacLeod, *Ain't No Makin' It*, 115.

6 MacLeod, *Ain't No Makin' It*, 51–4.

7 MacLeod, *Ain't No Makin' It*, 54–60.

8 MacLeod, *Ain't No Makin' It*, 179.

MODULE 6
SECONDARY IDEAS

KEY POINTS

- Jay MacLeod's secondary focus in *Ain't No Makin' It* is on the role the education system plays in maintaining social inequality* in the United States. Additionally, he focuses on the role that racism* plays in the lives of the group members.
- MacLeod says that schools serve to maintain class* differences in capitalist* society. He says schools should acknowledge the feelings and experiences of working-class children,* so they don't blame themselves when they don't achieve as much as their peers from the more affluent classes.
- Reaction to the book has generally been positive, but critics have tended to gloss over MacLeod's Marxist* analysis of the school system as a tool for maintaining the class system in America.

Other Ideas

Several secondary ideas emerge in Jay MacLeod's *Ain't No Makin' It*. MacLeod is interested in all of the social and institutional influences that determine how social inequality is passed on from generation to generation. He addresses these social influences and unifies his argument throughout by primarily looking at social reproduction* and achievement ideology.*

MacLeod deduces that the educational system plays a role in maintaining social inequality in a capitalist economy. He argues that the system merely maintains or even reduces the aspirations of poor urban youth. This is in line with the views of other scholars, who also

> "The present study shows quite clearly that neither race nor class can be reduced to abstract forces that mechanically manipulate people like electrons in a charged field. Rather, race and class (along with gender) are interwoven in variable patterns, and the resultant geometry is complex. Class and race work simultaneously, and each can magnify or mitigate the effects of the others."
>
> Jay MacLeod, *Ain't No Makin' It: Aspirations and Attainment in a Low-Income Neighborhood*

argue that schools play a role in reproducing social inequality from generation to generation. Using the case study of Lincoln High School, where the Brothers and the Hallway Hangers attend (or indeed avoid) classes, MacLeod demonstrates that the state-funded high school reduces students' opportunities for success in the workplace by lowering their already reduced aspirations.*

Another secondary theme in the book is the role that racism plays in the group members' lives. As an almost entirely black group, the Brothers experience racism from the Hallway Hangers and society at large throughout the study. As young men, the Brothers do not see race as a barrier to their success, believing that the civil rights* advances won by their parents and grandparents created a level playing field. Over time, however, the Brothers encounter racism in the workplace, discrimination finding jobs, and lack of access to the kinds of personal connections that MacLeod finds are key in securing entry-level service jobs. As they age, the Brothers acknowledge that racism *has* been an obstacle to their success. In the same way that constraints are caused by class,* racism limits the Brothers' opportunities.

Even so, like almost all Americans the Hallway Hangers and the Brothers "tend to interpret their situation in individual rather than structural* terms."[1] The Brothers do not see race as a limiting factor in their youth, and view their failures as the result of their own shortcomings. For their part, the Hallway Hangers have a very different understanding of the role of race. They "complain not about class oppression but about discrimination against white men."[2]

Exploring the Ideas

Theories of social reproduction argue that the relationships between students, teachers, and administrators "reflect those of the capitalist mode of production"[3] and the system of education in the United States "tailors the self-concepts,* [awareness and understanding of one's self as an individual], aspirations, and social class … of individuals to the requirements of the social division of labor."*[4] In other words, schools in capitalist economies train individuals to be members of capitalist societies, and to occupy the same position in it as their parents. Yet at the same time schools promote achievement ideology, promising success for hard work and promoting education as a certain way of achieving a better life.

MacLeod argues that the standard achievement ideology in schools should be replaced with "ways of motivating students that acknowledge rather than deny their social condition."[5] This change would see teachers accept the "legitimacy and importance of the students' feelings, perceptions, and experiences as working-class kids."[6] By acknowledging the *structural* conditions that create inequality, students can be freed from the psychological burden of blaming themselves for their position and lack of achievements in their future working lives. At the same time, this approach would help both teachers and students think about political and critical ways of addressing the policies and social behaviors that maintain this social inequality.

MacLeod investigates the role that race and racism play in the lives of both groups. He states that despite the huge gains of the Civil Rights Movement, racial inequality is actually built into the structure of American society. Racial inequality and social inequality are related to one another. "Neither race nor class can be reduced to abstract forces ... Rather, race and class (along with gender) are interwoven" in the lifetime experiences of the urban poor.[7] During his study, MacLeod found that the young Brothers did not feel race to be a barrier to their success, seemingly because they still embraced achievement ideology and believed that American society is open, fair, and upwardly mobile. The Hallway Hangers, on the other hand, do not see American society in such rosy terms and accurately perceive that their opportunities are limited. However, because they lack the knowledge and skills to evaluate the social structures* that restrict them, the Hallway Hangers turn to bitter racism against blacks. The Brothers, meanwhile, experience the effects of racial discrimination throughout their lives, and they gradually lower their optimistic teenager aspirations.[8] MacLeod argues that race and class are interrelated, each with social repercussions that are both objective (i.e. limited job opportunities) and subjective (i.e. negative attitudes about race).

Overlooked

Academic and public response to *Ain't No Makin' It* when it was first published was generally positive. That said, many reviews tended to overlook MacLeod's blunt criticism of the American economic structure and educational system. Most academic reviewers note some aspect of MacLeod's commitment to social justice,* but overall focus more intensely on the length of MacLeod's study or the shortcomings in his theory and interpretation.

However, by highlighting the structural causes of social inequality, MacLeod also pointed to potential areas for policy reform. He did not expect the problem would be solved quickly: "[the] transformation of American class society is currently a political impossibility and progressive social change is bound to be slow and piecemeal."[9] The state of youth and children living in poverty in the United States today is still bleak with 22 percent of all children living in this condition.[10] Almost half of black children under the age of six live in poverty.[11] These children attend schools that are overcrowded, underfunded, and understaffed. MacLeod's study, despite being highly influential in the field of sociology, did not spur widespread educational or economic reform. It was, however, an early voice in a gathering chorus speaking out in favor of a closer look at the structural causes of poverty, racism, and social inequality in the United States. Scholars continue this work today, developing new approaches to questions of social inequality. Sadly, MacLeod's contribution to the pursuit of social and economic justice* has been in the main overlooked by the general public.

NOTES

1 Jay MacLeod, *Ain't No Makin' It: Aspirations and Attainment in a Low-Income Neighborhood* (Boulder, Colorado: Westview Press, 2009), 252.

2 MacLeod, *Ain't No Makin' It,* 252.

3 MacLeod, *Ain't No Makin' It,* 12.

4 Samuel Bowles and Herbert Gintis, *Schooling in Capitalist America* (New York: Basic Books, 1976), 56.

5 MacLeod, *Ain't No Makin' It,* 264.

6 MacLeod, *Ain't No Makin' It,* 265.

7 MacLeod, *Ain't No Makin' It,* 250.

8 MacLeod, *Ain't No Makin' It,* 250.

9 MacLeod, *Ain't No Makin' It,* 266.

10 National Center for Children in Poverty, "Child Poverty," *National Center for Children in Poverty,* accessed September 30, 2015, http://www.nccp.org/topics/childpoverty.html.

11 The State of Working America, "Poverty," *The State of Working America,* accessed September 30, 2015, http://stateofworkingamerica.org/fact-sheets/poverty/.

MODULE 7
ACHIEVEMENT

KEY POINTS

- **Jay MacLeod provides substantial evidence that the structure of American society produces social inequality* that directly impacts the lifetime experience and achievements of the urban poor.**
- **The most significant factor in helping MacLeod reach this conclusion is his ability to make connections between sociological* theory and the individual experiences of the Brothers and the Hallway Hangers.**
- **While the book thoroughly explores the impact of class* and race, it does not look at gender relations* and the specific limits placed on working-class* and poor girls and women.**

Assessing the Argument

In *Ain't No Makin' It,* Jay MacLeod uses interviews and sociological theory to illustrate and support his conclusions. By following two groups of poor urban youth well into adulthood, he traces how their aspirations* impact them as they progress through life.

In part three of the 2009 edition, MacLeod presents the final set of interviews with members of both groups, all of whom are now in early middle age. By 2007 MacLeod found that, while "the majority of the men may still be mired at the bottom of society … some have achieved working-class stability and even penetrated the middle class."* In a poignant moment in the text, MacLeod is challenged by Isaac, a young, college-educated black man from the projects* who runs a health initiative for African American men. When MacLeod remarks to Isaac that "some of the men had even broken into the

> **“[W]e argue that the Brothers and Hallway Hangers have largely realized the predictions of a social reproduction approach. This perspective does not predict that all who start at the bottom will remain there; simply that the odds of succeeding, when one starts with next to nothing, are far lower than the achievement ideology would suggest ... It’s not that there “ain’t no makin’ it” at all ... it’s that the odds of getting there are long, and heavily dependent on luck and structural circumstances.”**
>
> Katherine McClelland and David Karen, “Analysis,” *Ain’t No Makin’ It: Aspirations and Attainment in a Low-Income Neighborhood*

middle class,” Isaac challenges him on the assumption implicit in the use of the word “even”: “We’re back blaming individuals rather than looking at the environment and the society. Your book taught me to resist this individualistic way of thinking that comes so naturally to most people. You haven’t forgotten the lessons of your own book, have you?” MacLeod honestly concludes: “Perhaps I had.”[1] In the final section of the text, MacLeod turns the analysis to Katherine McClelland* and David Karen,* sociologists themselves and MacLeod’s “friends, colleagues, and advisers ... since 1982.”[2] By doing so he offers the reader “fresh eyes and ears [that] have brought some fascinating insights.”[3]

McClelland and Karen present a summary, but also an evaluation, of MacLeod’s work. They focus on the achievements of both groups he interviewed as impacted by the job market, drugs, alcohol, and crime in the lives of the group members. They also look at race and racism,* family, mobility (or the lack thereof), religion, and political consciousness. They conclude that MacLeod’s understanding of how social reproduction* works is largely borne out by the life experiences of the members of both groups. Some individuals achieved middle-class status and a few began their own businesses. Social and economic achievements of the group members were influenced by their circumstances, by individual decisions, and by simple luck, with some individuals experiencing "dramatic turnarounds when the personal and structural circumstances are right."[4]

Achievement in Context

MacLeod was able to publish his research as *Ain't No Makin' It* shortly after submitting his senior thesis, and went on to produce two later editions of the text, each containing updated interviews. His study produced insights into how poverty is mainly the result of class inequality, and how that inequality is maintained over time. However, he concluded that it is not usually possible immediately and directly to change the social structures* that are responsible for maintaining this inequality. MacLeod's study did not, for example, spur radical reforms in inner-city schools or challenge Americans to rethink the unequal distribution of wealth* in the United States. And achievement ideology* remains a revered part of American culture, even as the wealth gap between rich and poor continues to grow to record proportions.

It is possible that MacLeod's research did not make a broader social or political impact simply because it presents too many challenges to the very structures of American society. It requires the reader to reassess some of the most basic ideas he or she has about American society. MacLeod puts some of the responsibility for making change happen on the shoulders of the reader, as well: "If the tide and toll of ... marginality in the United States is to be checked, new organizational forms of popular mobilization need to be nurtured: grassroots* organizations, women's groups, community organizing* outfits, and coalitions campaigning on issues of health, housing, schooling, childcare, crime, and local neighborhood concerns. Political parties and trade unions alone are ill-suited to stop the steady advance ... of social inequality."[5]

Limitations

A major limitation of the text is that it does not address either the experiences of girls or gender relations. Discussing why he did not focus more closely on gender relations, MacLeod explains that he "managed to stomach the racial prejudice of the Hallway Hangers and in striving to understand their racism came to see its cultural, political, and theoretical significance. Put off by their sexism, I missed an opportunity to understand it."[6] So *Ain't No Makin' It* offers a uniformly masculine outlook on life in "Clarendon Heights," even if the Hallway Hangers and the Brothers present two different understandings of masculinity, with completely opposing attitudes towards drugs, sex, school, and crime.

This text is relevant to everyone living in a capitalist* society. The influence of American capitalism has spread around the globe and most countries now operate on the basis of capitalist economies. Anyone interested in why social inequality exists in a society that claims to be economically open and upwardly mobile could gain valuable insight from reading *Ain't No Makin' It*. The book helps clarify how it is social structures, and not personal failings, that perpetuate inequality and poverty. Understanding how these structures function is key to developing strategies for creating more just and equal alternatives.

Since MacLeod began his studies in the 1980s, *Ain't No Makin' It* has also served as an ethnographic* account of this period of American history. So the book is relevant for historians and those who are interested in the individual stories from this era. It is also relevant to the fields of sociology, anthropology,* and economics.* The experiences of the Hallway Hangers and the Brothers show how social and economic structures directly impact individual lives.

NOTES

1 Jay MacLeod, *Ain't No Makin' It: Aspirations and Attainment in a Low-Income Neighborhood* (Boulder, Colorado: Westview Press, 2009), 408.

2 MacLeod, *Ain't No Makin' It*, 408.

3 MacLeod, *Ain't No Makin' It*, 408.

4 MacLeod, *Ain't No Makin' It*, 457.

5 MacLeod, *Ain't No Makin' It*, 269.

6 MacLeod, *Ain't No Makin' It*, 476.

MODULE 8
PLACE IN THE AUTHOR'S WORK

KEY POINTS

- *Ain't No Makin' It* comprises most of Jay MacLeod's academic thinking and encapsulates his life's scholarly work.
- MacLeod believes that sociology* reveals the truth about a society, and that revealing the truth about inequality* will help motivate people to work to change the structures* of a society that maintains inequality.
- MacLeod's reputation as a sociologist is based on his work in *Ain't No Makin' It*. But he wrote the book for the general public, and not just for a small community of scholars.

Positioning

Ain't No Makin' It: Aspirations and Attainment in a Low-Income Neighborhood represents Jay MacLeod's most significant contribution to understanding social inequality in the United States. The text has been published in three editions. The first, published in 1987 as *Ain't No Makin' It: Leveled Aspirations in a Low-Income Neighbourhood*, was MacLeod's undergraduate thesis research and it makes up part one of the third edition. Part two includes the interviews and MacLeod's interpretations when he returned to "Clarendon Heights" in 1991. Part three adds minimally edited interviews from 2006–7 and an analysis by two of MacLeod's colleagues and mentors, sociologists Katherine McClelland* and David Karen.* This means the text represents both MacLeod's first scholarly endeavor, as well as his academic life's work as it unfolded over the course of more than two decades.

> "*Ain't No Makin' It* will be of great interest to anyone seeking to understand how social inequality is reproduced. It does an excellent job of applying social reproduction theory to the real-life experiences of two youth groups; and the longitudinal nature of the study allows the reader to see how the ideas and thoughts formed early on can affect individuals much later in life. The next step is to apply these insights in an effort to achieve a greater degree of social justice."
>
> Nicolaus R. Espitia, "Review of *Ain't No Makin' It*," *Journal of Applied Social Science*

MacLeod produced other scholarship in the same subject area, though none of it was as successful or popular as *Ain't No Makin' It*. While working as a community organizer* in rural Mississippi, he published an article applying what he had learned completing *Ain't No Makin' It* to the question of how teachers can address socioeconomic* factors that limit success, and how to motivate youth. MacLeod began a youth oral history* project called Bloodlines, in which young local people interviewed veterans of the Civil Rights Movement* about their experiences. The findings of the Bloodlines project were published by MacLeod in 1991 as *Minds Stayed on Freedom: The Civil Rights Struggle in the Rural South: An Oral History.* Speaking about the relationship between social inequality and education, MacLeod argues that "as students develop tools of social analysis and begin to understand how inequities in wealth, power, and privilege affect them, this critical awareness of selfhood … becomes a motivating force much more powerful than the achievement ideology."*[1] A reader of *Ain't No Makin' It* will find that all of MacLeod's scholarship focuses on themes of wealth, power, and privilege.

Integration

It may be surprising to readers of *Ain't No Makin' It* that the author is now a parish priest. MacLeod's research and career choices reflect a commitment to respecting, listening to, and valuing the most vulnerable members of society, especially the poor. This connects his later career as a parish priest to his early sociological research as an undergraduate.

On one of his return interviews, MacLeod visits Chris, one of only two black members of the Hallway Hangers, in prison. Chris asks MacLeod about his faith and MacLeod responds: "My faith in a forgiving God allows me to face up to the truth about myself and to deal constructively with my sin. The United States is even more prone to self-deception than I am … sociology can help the world work through its ignorance of itself. Spirituality and sociology have parallel vocations. Spirituality reveals the truth about ourselves. Sociology reveals the truth about our society. Both spur us to struggle for justice, for in the end my redemption is linked to yours."[2] For MacLeod, justice and redemption are communal concepts, rather than individual ones. It is perhaps this same ethos that motivated a young Jay MacLeod to leave the wealth and privilege of Harvard University* to see what life was like for people on the poor side of town. It may also be what motivated him to return to interview the Hallway Hangers and the Brothers over the course of nearly 25 years. Taken together, MacLeod's work and career choices can be seen as a unified commitment to applying the ideas of sociology to the pursuit of social justice.*

Significance

Ain't No Makin' It is MacLeod's best-known and most significant work. The original study was groundbreaking and published in 1987 at a time when the topic of social inequality and, especially, the state of poor urban youth, had captured the attention of politicians, musicians, artists, and scholars alike.

Ain't No Makin' It solidified MacLeod's reputation as a sociologist. It is worth noting that he completed an undergraduate degree, but did not go on to do graduate study in a social science. MacLeod opted to attend theological school and became an ordained Anglican* priest. Later editions of the text added expanded interviews, refreshed analyses, and valuable insight into the long-term impacts of a youth spent in poverty. However, reviewers of the third edition also highlighted that MacLeod did not use developments in sociological theory to reinterpret his data over the long duration of the study. Instead, the theories MacLeod relied on for interpreting his data remained largely unchanged. Yet the strength of this text lies in the length of the study, the content of the interviews, the originality of MacLeod's original research questions, and in MacLeod's unswerving commitment to using his message to inspire social and educational reform.

Most of MacLeod's scholarship was published for the general public, not for a more limited academic readership. This reflects the type of scholarship MacLeod was interested in, but also his commitment to making his findings accessible to everyone. Both *Minds Stayed on Freedom* and *Ain't No Makin' It* focus on the long-term experiences of people who grew up oppressed by the social structures of poverty and race. In *Ain't No Makin' It,* the reader follows the lives of the Hallway Hangers and the Brothers. In *Minds Stayed on Freedom,* the reader learns about the struggles of civil rights activists as they are explained to a younger generation of African Americans.

NOTES

1 Jay MacLeod, "Bridging School and Street," *Journal of Negro Education* 60, no. 3 (1991): 274.

2 Jay MacLeod, *Ain't No Makin' It: Aspirations and Attainment in a Low-Income Neighborhood* (Boulder, Colorado: Westview Press, 2009), 504.

SECTION 3
IMPACT

MODULE 9
THE FIRST RESPONSES

KEY POINTS

- The most important criticism of *Ain't No Makin' It* is that Jay MacLeod never fully clarifies the relationship between individual autonomy (people's personal choices) and social structures* (for example, schools) in his interpretations of social inequality.*
- MacLeod made later additions to the text, adding more interviews, more interpretation, and some general suggestions as to how to apply his findings to social policy. However, he never responded directly to reviews of the work.
- *Ain't No Makin' It* is now considered a classic work of American sociology* and is widely assigned in sociology courses.

Criticism

Responses to Jay MacLeod's *Ain't No Makin' It* were largely positive. The third edition, significantly expanded from the first edition in 1987 which was subtitled *Leveled Aspirations in a Low-Income Neighborhood,* was published in 2009. This means that responses to the book span more than two decades.

The first review of the book appeared in the *American Journal of Sociology*, where it was praised as "an exciting book—provocative in what it includes, tantalizing in what it leaves out, frustrating in what remains ambiguous."[1] This review reflects many of the subsequent reviews, which are positive overall, but which also flag up areas for future development. In the same review, Harvard* sociologist Jennifer Hochschild (then at Princeton) feels it is inadequate that MacLeod

> **"This book [*Ain't No Makin' It*] represents a masterful exercise in reconstituting the critical questions about the interconnection of race, class, gender, and experience ... The fact that his work raises the right questions is of greater importance than his inability to answer them fully. It is the job of sociologists ... to read this book and to take the unresolved questions as a platform for further inquiry."**
>
> Alford A. Young, "Review of *Ain't No Makin' It*," *American Journal of Sociology*

"tries to deal with the fact that *his* black subjects are so different [from other black urban youth] through a few (too brief) comments."[2] On the other hand, Hochschild finds MacLeod's idea more convincing that the boys' behavior at school is guided by what they learn from their family lives. MacLeod points out in his appendix that he simply did not have time for the fieldwork he intended to do in schools and homes. Nevertheless, Hochschild finds the school and family remain "straw figures" and, as such, the connection between individual autonomy and social structure is never fully clarified.

Responses

Each publication of an updated edition of *Ain't No Makin' It: Aspirations and Attainment in a Low-Income Neighborhood* was reviewed, especially in sociology journals. In most cases, the reviews were positive—and blurbs from many of the positive reviews are included in the third edition. Interestingly, Jay MacLeod did not respond directly to published reviews of any of the three editions. This could be because his focus throughout this period was on other matters.

MacLeod was a Rhodes scholar* the year he graduated from Harvard. He then moved to rural Mississippi and became a community organizer.* In 1991, he published *Minds Stayed on Freedom* based on interviews conducted by youth in Mississippi. MacLeod then made a long-term move to England, his wife's native country, to attend Lincoln Theological College in Lincolnshire, before becoming a parish priest. In 2013, he returned to the US to become rector (parish priest) at Saint Andrew's Episcopal Church in New London, Connecticut. It appears that MacLeod's long-term career decisions, at least since the early 1990s, have been focused on serving his faith community.

That said, MacLeod continued to interview the Hallway Hangers and the Brothers. A reviewer of the second edition of his book published in 1995 noted that MacLeod had responded to the call for "follow up research ... further theoretical explication of the findings ... and more explicit attention to how such work may facilitate the formation of public policy."[3] If MacLeod adjusted his research questions, methods, or interpretations to address some of the shortcomings in his research, as pointed out by his reviewers, he makes no mention of it in the text. This lack of engagement with the broader field of sociology, where his book made a big impact, seems odd from an academic point of view. But it makes sense if we think of MacLeod as a social reformer who maintained his professional and personal commitment to his early research while pursuing a career outside of academia.

Conflict and Consensus

In 2009, MacLeod published the third edition of *Ain't No Makin' It*. As with previous editions, reviews of the text generally restated its significance within the field of sociology, while continuing to point out areas ripe for further development. In that year, MacLeod appeared at the annual meeting of the *American Sociological Association* in Boston, Massachusetts to sign copies of the third edition of *Ain't No Makin' It*. According to Susan Ferguson, a sociologist at Grinnell College, "to people like us, MacLeod is a celebrity. His book has been taught in college classrooms for more than 20 years—and for good reason … it is in many ways a perfect introduction for any reader to the limited opportunities for mobility and success faced by many Americans, and the consequences of our continuing inability or unwillingness to see and understand these realities."[4] The widespread use of MacLeod's text in college classrooms in both anthropology* and sociology departments is evidence of his study's lasting impact. On the other hand, many reviewers point out that there is still much work to be done in applying MacLeod's insights to the reform of the social structures that limit success for the poor. Given his career choices and his statement that the third edition of *Ain't No Makin' It* is the final edition, it seems that the work of applying MacLeod's insights to meaningful educational and social reform falls to the current generation of scholars.

NOTES

1 Jennifer L. Hochschild, "Review of *Ain't No Makin' It: Leveled Aspirations in a Low-Income Neighborhood* by Jay McLeod," *American Journal of Sociology* 94, no. 1 (1988): 182.

2 Hochschild, "Review," 183.

3 Alford A. Young Jr., "Review of *Ain't No Makin' It: Aspirations and Attainment in a Low-Income Neighborhood* by Jay McLeod," *American Journal of Sociology* 101, no. 6 (1996): 1758–60.

4 Susan J. Ferguson, "Still No Makin' It: Review of *Ain't No Makin' It: Aspirations and Attainment in a Low-Income Neighborhood* by Jay McLeod," *Contexts* 8 (2009): 74.

MODULE 10
THE EVOLVING DEBATE

KEY POINTS

- **The most important impact made by Jay MacLeod's study has been to turn the spotlight away from the (often problematic) responses of the urban poor and on to the actual structures* within American society that create and pass on social inequality.***
- **By focusing on institutional barriers to social advancement, MacLeod's study and those it inspired generated a school of thought that challenges a core part of the American Dream:* the notion that anyone can be a success through hard work.**
- **MacLeod's work helped pave the way for later studies by demonstrating that investigations of social structures themselves can yield insight into social inequality.**

Uses and Problems

In *Ain't No Makin' it: Aspirations and Attainment in a Low-Income Neighborhood,* Jay MacLeod relies on the theory of social reproduction* to look at how class* structure in the United States is being perpetuated from generation to generation. He also evaluates the degree to which the educational system as experienced by the Hallway Hangers and the Brothers flattens their aspirations.* As a form of Marxist* theory, social reproduction argues that "schools are not institutions of equal opportunity but mechanisms for perpetuating social inequalities,"[1] essentially by preparing pupils to occupy the same status as their parents in the class system. This approach was most popular in the field of sociology* between the 1960s and the 1990s. MacLeod used social reproduction theory in the final decade of its popularity.

> **"A rigid cause (lack of social capital) and effect (problem behaviors) framework obscures the fact that youth in poor communities in the United States and abroad utilize agency and self-determination to make healthy choices and participate in civic engagement and sometimes radical and revolutionary change."**
>
> A. A. Akom et al., *Youthtopias: Towards a New Paradigm of Critical Youth Studies*

Nevertheless, MacLeod's study is one of many that focus on how the circumstances of poverty experienced by urban youth restrict their aspirations and achievements. This interpretive approach used by scholars has changed over time. In particular, sociological studies in the 1980s tended to focus on problematic, disruptive, or nonconformist behavior. MacLeod himself acknowledges this in the text: "Nonconformity fascinates the sociologist, and if in this book undue attention is given to … the Hallway Hangers [it is because they] undergo the process of social reproduction in a unique fashion."[2] Over time, however, sociological studies have shifted away from models of social reproduction, nonconformity, and social capital* to understand how youth make decisions and express individual agency* (the ability to act on one's choices), despite their circumstances. This newer approach, known as critical youth studies,* focuses on how young people analyze their circumstances, how they understand and critique social structures, and how they can and do actively resist oppression.[3]

Schools of Thought

MacLeod's approach can be said to be Marxist* (focusing on issues of class in American society), structural* (focused on social structures such as schools), and dialectical* (concerned with the relationship between individuals and social structures). In many ways, these approaches characterized the practice of sociology in the United States in the 1980s.[4] The publication of *Ain't No Makin' It* in 1987 influenced thinking both in the field of sociology and among the broader American public. Many readers were surprised that of the two groups MacLeod studied—one violent, nonconformist, drug using, with low hopes for their future, the other responsible, hardworking, and with high expectations—the nonconformist group was mostly white and the hardworking group was mostly black. For this reason, MacLeod's work was significant in challenging popular assumptions about race, poverty, and violence.

MacLeod also contributed to a school of thought looking to investigate the role social structures play in maintaining socioeconomic* inequality. MacLeod's work was positively received and helped generate momentum for similar critical studies. As one reviewer put it: "Any study questioning the United States' enormously powerful achievement ideology* is commendable, particularly one that demonstrates the consequences of deindustrialization and deteriorating social institutions for the aspirations, ideologies, and attainments of urban youth."[5]

By challenging something as fundamental as the American Dream, MacLeod demonstrated that no part of American ideology was beyond evaluation and study. He also drew attention to the growing gap between rich and poor in the United States. This has been of particular interest to activists, scholars, politicians, economists, and the American public in recent years, as evidenced by the grassroots* protest movement Occupy Wall Street* that drew attention to global inequality in 2011. This has at least led to continuing discussion and debate about social and economic inequality in the United States and around the world.

In Current Scholarship

Today, the field of critical youth studies continues the work of evaluating the relationship between individual agency and the social structures that maintain socioeconomic inequality. Critical youth studies sit in "an emergent tradition of scholarship that privileges a more self-conscious and critical mode of inquiry and analysis ... and also redress[es] ... the power imbalance inherent in doing qualitative research with youth by conducting non-exploitative and more reflexive* researches ... Youth are brought actively into the research process as creative agents."[6] This contrasts with MacLeod's approach, in which youth were the subject of the study, but were not invited to actively participate in shaping the research project. By inviting youth to help shape research questions, formulate solutions, and address the behaviors and structures that limit their success, critical youth studies reflects an attempt to empower youth to take active roles in their own communities and society.

Like MacLeod, scholars in critical youth studies continue to focus on educational solutions. Specifically, the creation of traditional and nontraditional educational settings for young people offers them ways of building on their existing cultural capital* and social capital.* Scholars who are pursuing these solutions point out that, in searching for what is problematic or dysfunctional in poor urban communities, theorists "miss genuine love, humor, academic achievement, nontraditional families, positive relationships towards men, women and children, and all kinds of social and cultural capital that is alive, well, and thriving in black and brown urban communities that is presently flying under the radar."[7] By focusing on their potential and the cultural knowledge these people already possess, and by tailoring curriculum to the real needs of young people, these scholars continue the work of creating social and economic justice* for all Americans.

NOTES

1 James Collins, "Social Reproduction in Classrooms and Schools," *Annual Review of Anthropology* 38 (2009): 33.

2 Jay MacLeod, *Ain't No Makin' It: Aspirations and Attainment in a Low-Income Neighborhood* (Boulder, Colorado: Westview Press, 2009), 45.

3 A. A. Akom et al., "Youthtopias: Towards a New Paradigm of Critical Youth Studies," *Youth Media Reporter: The Professional Journal of the Youth Media Field* 2, no. 4 (2008), accessed September 30, 2105, http://iseeed.org/wp-content/uploads/2012/12/Akom_Youthtopias-YMR-Article.pdf.

4 M. S. A. Rao, "Sociology in the 1980s," *Economic and Political Weekly* 14, no. 44 (1979): 1810–15.

5 Deirdre Royster, "Review of *Ain't No Makin' It: Aspirations and Attainment in a Low-Income Neighborhood* by Jay MacLeod," *Contemporary Sociology* 25, no. 2 (1996): 151.

6 Mattia Fumanti, "Review of 'Representing Youth: Methodological Issues in Critical Youth Studies' by Amy L. Best," *Journal of the Royal Anthropological Institute* 15, no. 4 (2009): 876.

7 Akom et al., "Youthtopias," 9–10.

MODULE 11
IMPACT AND INFLUENCE TODAY

KEY POINTS

- Today, *Ain't No Makin' It* is viewed as a classic text in American sociology* and is widely assigned in sociology and anthropology* courses.
- Criticisms of the book have mainly focused on three areas—the need for follow-up study, for more specific policy recommendations and for more clarity on the relation between observations and theory.
- Today, scholars use approaches such as critical youth studies* to propose ideas for how to educate youth about structural inequality* in the United States to develop political and social awareness, increase individual agency* (the ability to act freely based on personal choice), and build on the strengths of local communities.

Position

Jay MacLeod's *Ain't No Makin' It: Aspirations and Attainment in a Low-Income Neighborhood* is still widely assigned in sociology courses. It provides an excellent introduction to the field of sociology, the application of ethnographic* methods, and is situated in the intersection between social justice* and academic study. Because *Ain't No Makin' It* was first published almost 30 years ago, it is no longer the focus of academic debates, but is still seen as a classic in the field of sociology.

The most important impact of this text is to highlight the role that poverty, rather than personal failure, plays in restricting the life ambitions and achievements of the urban poor. By highlighting social inequality,* rather than racial difference or personal shortcomings,

> **"[I]n following the fates of these young men, MacLeod provides a brilliant, nuanced account of lives devoid of any hope of a stable life, and the near total wastage of young men caught in the grips of a deindustrializing economy. This is anthropology at its very best, an engaged and committed social science probing the most crucial of fault lines."**
>
> Katherine Newman, "Review of *Ain't No Makin' It*," *American Ethnologist*

MacLeod helped turn the spotlight away from the urban poor on to the structures that *maintain* social inequality in the United States. The influence of this idea led the journal *Contemporary Sociology* to include *Ain't No Makin' It* in a list of books that should "be found in the sociology section of ... local bookstores."[1] MacLeod's work is on this list alongside such classics as political economist Karl Marx's* *The Communist Manifesto,** sociologist Émile Durkheim's* *The Elementary Forms of Religious Life,** and sociologist and economist Max Weber's* *The Protestant Ethic and the Spirit of Capitalism** and *Economy and Society.** Scholars have continued to build on MacLeod's ideas, using different approaches to the question of social inequality, and looking for "real world", practical solutions to creating genuinely equal opportunity.

Interaction

Many of the reviews of *Ain't No Makin' It* were positive. They highlighted how useful the text was for teaching and acknowledged MacLeod's status in the field of sociology. Reviewing the third edition, sociologist Susan J. Ferguson remarked that MacLeod has celebrity-like status within the field and that "the book's continuing appeal and import goes well beyond sociology classrooms and pedagogy* [the study and practice of effective teaching]. It is, in many ways, a perfect introduction to the limited opportunities and mobility and success faced by many Americans and the consequences of our continuing inability or unwillingness to see and understand these realities."[2]

When reviewers pointed out shortcomings of MacLeod's study, they focused on three main areas, calling for follow-up research, further clarification of the relationship between MacLeod's observations and his theories, and for more explicit information about how MacLeod's findings could be used to inform public policy.[3]

Although he did not engage directly with any of the criticisms, in subsequent editions MacLeod addressed each of these areas, returning for additional interviews with the Brothers and the Hallway Hangers in their twenties and in their forties, all the time making connections between social reproduction* and potential areas for reform. In the second edition, MacLeod uses the same theoretical framework to evaluate why the Brothers and Hangers succeeded or failed in the job market. He finds that both groups "have been stuck … with low wages, infrequent raises, awkward working hours, minimal training, and high turnover"[4] and he argues more passionately for educational and social reform. For the third edition, MacLeod turns the analysis over to sociologists Katherine McClelland* and David Karen,* who provide a new perspective.

The Continuing Debate

Critics of MacLeod's work identified that his attempt to clarify the connection between individual agency and social structure was only partially successful. By the third edition, it can be seen that the adults who were part of the Hallway Hangers and the Brothers share many of the same problems. They have difficulty finding employment, and have personal struggles with drugs and alcohol, racism,* and violent behavior. MacLeod's study demonstrates trends in how poverty shapes the lives of the Hallway Hangers and the Brothers, but cannot completely account for the individual achievements of the group members who have more success in life.

Even though MacLeod dedicated a section of his final chapter in the second edition to how his study could impact public policy, "... he offers what are by now very traditional criticisms of the way in which public institutions ineffectively respond to the needs and interests of low-income citizens ... what is needed here is a multilevel strategic platform for institutional change."[5] As is the case with large-scale social challenges—poverty, social inequality, racism, etc.—it is often easier to shine a light on the structural causes of these conditions than it is to put forward or implement solutions. MacLeod offers only general suggestions as to how to reform schools and American society.

Critical youth studies address some of the same questions as MacLeod from the perspective of the agency of youth, or how young people exercise individual choice within the constraints of social structures. Scholars focus on "new kinds of spaces where resistance and resiliency can be developed through formal (and informal) processes, pedagogical structures, and youth cultural practice" as a step "vital towards creating a movement of social justice* and equality."[6] Doing so involves a major shift that builds on approaches such as MacLeod's, but with a critical focus on developing educational settings that empower young people to understand and change the very structures of social inequality.

NOTES

1 Contemporary Sociology, "Books mentioned multiple times on lists of books, which we would like to see in the sociology section of our local bookstores," *Contemporary Sociology* 28 (1999): 159.

2 Susan J. Ferguson, "Still No Makin' It: Review of *Ain't No Makin' It: Aspirations and Attainment in a Low-Income Neighborhood* by Jay McLeod," *Contexts* 8 (2009): 74.

3 Alford A. Young Jr., "Review of *Ain't No Makin' It: Aspirations and Attainment in a Low-Income Neighborhood* by Jay McLeod," *American Journal of Sociology* 101, no. 6 (1996): 1758.

4 Jay MacLeod, *Ain't No Makin' It: Aspirations and Attainment in a Low-Income Neighborhood* (Boulder, Colorado: Westview Press, 2009), 245.

5 Young, "Review," 1759.

6 A. A. Akom et al., "Youthtopias: Towards a New Paradigm of Critical Youth Studies," *Youth Media Reporter: The Professional Journal of the Youth Media Field* 2, no. 4 (2008): 2, accessed September 30, 2105, http://iseeed.org/wp-content/uploads/2012/12/Akom_Youthtopias-YMR-Article.pdf.

MODULE 12
WHERE NEXT?

KEY POINTS

- *Ain't No Makin' It* will continue to be a classic text in sociology.*
- By drawing attention to the structural causes of social inequality* in the United States, the text helped set the stage for the recent rise of critical youth studies.*
- With its surprisingly human portrait of the sometimes anti-social young men it follows, the text challenges simplistic ideas of the relationship between urban poverty, race, education, violence, socioeconomic* achievement, and the economic structure of American society.

Potential

Ain't No Makin' It will continue to be relevant to readers in the fields of sociology,* anthropology,* studies of race, social policy, and economics.* It is considered a cornerstone text and is widely assigned in sociology and anthropology courses. Its status ensures that scholars will continue to make use of the book. New questions, new approaches, and new solutions will continue to come up in the United States and around the globe as long as social inequality* persists. *Ain't No Makin' It* shows that some of the members of the Hallway Hangers and the Brothers attained middle-class* status by starting their own businesses. As one reviewer noted: "as manufacturing jobs continue to be lost, and federal and state governments continue to develop programs to encourage entrepreneurial activity … to diversify the economy … it will be interesting to see if there will be an increase in upward mobility* or if the established resources will be set aside for those already in the upper or middle class."[1]

> **“In short, what is required is the creation of a truly open society—a society where the life chances of those at the bottom are not radically different from those at the top and where wealth is distributed more equitably. The socialist vision of a transformed class structure that radically reduces social inequality may seem hopelessly out of touch, but there is no denying that the capitalist free market, left to itself, can neither protect the environment nor meet human needs.”**
>
> Jay MacLeod, *Ain't No Makin' It: Aspirations and Attainment in a Low-Income Neighborhood*

Social inequality between the rich and the poor has grown to even higher levels than when MacLeod first published *Ain't No Makin' It* in 1987. Inequality in wages, homelessness, racial and gender discrimination, racial gaps in education, child poverty, a lack of jobs that pay a living wage, and the disproportionate numbers of ethnic minorities sent to prison, remain serious problems in American society, as well as in other places around the world. Understanding the structural* roots of these inequalities, and developing political and practical solutions to create social justice,* remain pressing challenges. MacLeod's text will continue to be important because of the subject matter it tackles and because it is a core text in the field. New solutions and approaches can be built from it.

Future Directions

Today, the development of critical youth studies—focusing not only on the limiting and damaging structures of social inequality that impact poor youth, but also on the resilience, resistance, and agency* of youth—present an exciting development in how to approach and address issues of social inequality. Other areas that are still being developed are the investigation of specific institutions and policies and their role in perpetuating social inequality. For example, the soaring tuition fees in the American and Canadian university systems, and the expansion of for-profit professional higher education, have changed the experience of university for students. The university system, notes one scholar, is structured to "convince those who do not [do] well to blame themselves for their failures rather than the system that orchestrates these failures."[2] If this interpretation sounds familiar, it is because these and other current scholars continue to share MacLeod's concerns with questions of inequality, social structure,* and individual agency.

Critical youth studies rely on existing theories of social or cultural capital* to study the role that location within an urban space plays in employment prospects,[3] the use of sports to promote urban regeneration and social renewal within communities,[4] and the creation of urban youth languages as a form of cultural and social capital that can bridge ethnic difference.[5] Critical youth studies is an exciting development that combines anthropological, sociological, and economic approaches to addressing issues of socioeconomic inequality with a clear focus on empowering youth.

Summary

Ain't No Makin' It is a classic text in the field of sociology that is also relevant to anthropology, economics, the study of race and racism,* social policy, and educational and economic reform. Readers interested in social inequality, social reproduction,* and the role of the educational system in perpetuating cycles of poverty will enjoy this book. The book is also valuable for its humanizing portrayal of what were considered to be some of America's most marginalized, disadvantaged people. Here the reader learns that the urban poor are not fundamentally different from anyone else. They simply have access to very limited resources. *Ain't No Makin' It* gives them voice.

In a decade that was characterized by extreme wealth alongside growing poverty, what was an all-time-high gap between the rich and the poor, with federal policy that both cut services for the urban poor and labeled them as morally inferior to the middle and upper class, MacLeod's study stood out as a well-reasoned criticism of many widely held popular assumptions. MacLeod's key point—that it is social structures that limit individual achievement, not individual failures—has a strong message for all social institutions. By drawing attention to the role the educational system plays in continuing to perpetuate social and economic inequality in a capitalist* economy, MacLeod also highlights the importance of serious educational reform as critical to creating true conditions of social equality.

NOTES

1 Nicolaus R. Espitia, "Review of *Ain't No Makin' It: Aspirations and Attainment in a Low-Income Neighborhood* by Jay MacLeod," *Journal of Applied Social Science* 3 (2009): 81–4.

2 James Côté and Anton Allahar, "Response to 'Anxious Academics: Mission Drift and Sliding Standards in the Modern Canadian University,'" *Canadian Journal of Sociology* 33, no. 2 (2008): 1072.

3 Katherine M. O'Regan and John M. Quigley, "Where Youth Live: Economic Effects of Urban Space on Employment Prospects," *Urban Studies* 35, no. 7 (1998): 1187–205.

4 Ramón Spaaij et al., "Urban Youth, Worklessness and Sport: A Comparison of Sports-based Employability Programmes in Rotterdam and Stoke-on Trent," *Urban Studies* 50, no. 8 (2013): 1608–24.

5 Roland Kiessling and Maarten Mous, "Urban Youth Languages in Africa," *Anthropological Linguistics* 46, no. 3 (2004): 303–41.

GLOSSARY

GLOSSARY OF TERMS

Achievement ideology: a socially constructed belief that hard work is rewarded with economic and social success. The American Dream is an example of achievement ideology.

Agency: the ability with which an individual can act freely, based on personal choice. The idea of agency is relevant to social sciences such as sociology, anthropology, and economics.

American Dream: an American form of achievement ideology stating that the United States is a land of equal opportunities that are accessible to all citizens through hard work. The American Dream is based on the possibility of upward mobility and the claim that there are few obstacles to attaining financial and social success in the United States.

Anglican: a branch of Christianity comprising the Church of England. The beliefs and practices of Anglicans represent a theological middle ground between Roman Catholicism and Protestantism.

Anthropology: the study of humankind, including the evolution of the human species, the prehistoric record of humanity, languages, and social and cultural phenomena.

Aspirations: an individual's hopes and understanding of his or her social and economic future. From a sociological perspective, aspirations represent the compromise an individual makes between their wishes and the structural limitations they confront.

Capitalism: an economic and social system in which private owners, not the government, control the production and trade of material goods. Capitalist economies are characterized by the concepts of private ownership of property, the accumulation of wealth, and a competitive market focused on profit.

Civil Rights Movement: a social and political movement in the 1950s and 1960s dedicated to ending racial segregation through acts of peaceful protest and, when necessary, civil disobedience.

Class or social class: a person's place within the hierarchy of social and economic wealth, often divided into the upper, middle, and lower classes.

Class inequality: unequal access to education, wealth, jobs, health care, and other resources due to a person's class.

***The Communist Manifesto*:** originally published by Karl Marx and Friedrich Engels in 1848, this pamphlet presented an analysis of the conflict between social classes and an evaluation of the social problems caused by a capitalist economy.

Community organizer: a professional who works to organize individuals in developing strategies for improving the social, economic, and political conditions of their community. Community organizers typically help poor communities to have a voice in the policies that impact them.

Contextualize: to view data with regard to broader social and cultural contexts or theories in order to improve understanding.

Counterculture: a group of individuals who share values that are often in opposition, or counter, to mainstream cultural or social values.

Critical youth studies: a developing area of scholarship focused on how youth exercise individual agency to make decisions within their social circumstances. Critical youth studies focus on the cultural resources of the community, positive community assets, and what is working well in the community, not just what is failing.

Cultural capital: first proposed by Pierre Bourdieu, the idea that non-financial cultural assets also have value in society and, therefore, can function as a kind of cultural currency. Examples of forms of cultural capital include education and manner of speech, physical appearance, including racial appearance, and style of dressing.

Deterministic: deterministic models in the social sciences, especially sociology, argue that individual humans do not have much agency (or choice) within social structures and, instead, that the lifetime outcomes of individuals are determined by the structures of society itself.

Dialectical: generally, an approach that relies on argument and discussion to solve problems. In anthropology or sociology, a dialectical approach is concerned with the relationship and feedback between social, economic, and cultural factors.

Distribution of wealth: the manner in which wealth is proportionately distributed through a society.

Economic capital: according to Bourdieu, economic capital is one of four kinds of capital, or economic resources. Economic capital is wealth or money. It can be contrasted to cultural, social, or symbolic capital, which cannot be assigned monetary value but still make meaningful financial impacts.

Economic justice: a set of ethically motivated theories and practices dedicated to ensuring that all people have adequate financial resources (including jobs) in order to live freely, regardless of their socioeconomic class.

Economics: a social science focused on the study of how human societies produce, distribute, and consume material and cultural resources via different systems of exchange.

***Economy and Society*:** a book by Max Weber published posthumously in 1922, viewed as a foundational text in sociology.

***The Elementary Forms of Religious Life*:** a key sociological text published by Émile Durkheim in 1912. In this text, Durkheim investigated the nature, purpose, and origin of religion to evaluate religion as a social behavior.

Ethnography: an anthropological approach in which the beliefs, behaviors, and customs of individuals or cultures are studied and described.

Gender relations: the social, cultural, and economic relationships between male and female persons within a society.

Grassroots movement: a social or political movement in which ordinary people, as opposed to politicians, make up the membership of the group.

Habitus: a term first proposed by French sociologist Pierre Bourdieu, habitus is used to describe a system of attitudes, beliefs, perceptions, and experiences that are shared by members of the same group or class.

Harvard University: a prestigious American research institution established in 1636. The oldest institution of higher education in the United States, Harvard is also known to routinely hold the largest financial endowment of any university in the world.

Human capital: the knowledge, habits, and personal attributes that an individual may apply toward his/her work in order to achieve economic success.

Ideology: a system of beliefs or understandings held by an individual person or a group that are used to make sense of the world. Most members of a culture will share certain ideologies: the American Dream and capitalism are two common ideologies in American society.

Informants: an anthropological term used to identify individuals from whom an anthropologist receives information in a field setting.

Labor system: the structure by which labor is organized and controlled within a capitalist society and economy.

Lincoln Theological College: a theological college in Lincolnshire, England that offered training and ordination to Anglican priests. The college closed in 1995 due to declining numbers of theological students seeking ordinations.

Linguistics: the scientific study of the form, meaning, and sociocultural context of language.

Longitudinal studies: observational research projects in which data is collected on the same participants over an extended period of time.

Mainstream: beliefs or behaviors that are viewed as being "normal" within a society. In general, mainstream ideas are shared broadly throughout a culture and are reflected in trends in politics, art, fashion, and music.

Marxist: influenced by the theories of Karl Marx, Marxist approaches focus on understanding conflicts between social classes and the structures of social and economic production.

Middle class: the social class between the upper and lower classes, the middle class is difficult to define in objective terms. The historic ideology of the middle class is part of the American Dream: lower-class people believe that hard work will allow them to move out of poor circumstances into the relative comfort of the middle class.

Occupy Wall Street: a grassroots protest movement in the United States that drew attention to global social and economic inequality, especially the extreme gap between the rich and the poor. The protest began when protestors occupied Zuccotti Park in New York City on September 17, 2011.

Oral history: history that is transmitted through oral storytelling and interviews, not through written texts. Oral history often captures the rich details of personal experience that are not found in broader historical overviews.

Oxford University: the second oldest existing university in the world, Oxford University in Oxford, England, is known for its academic excellence. Oxford University is home to the Rhodes scholarship, one of the most prestigious scholarships in the world.

Pedagogy: the study, theory, and methods of effective teaching and educational practices.

Poverty line: a federally defined threshold for household poverty. In the United States in 2015, the poverty line was defined as $24,250 for a family of four.

***The Protestant Ethic and the Spirit of Capitalism*:** a key sociological text published by Max Weber in 1905. The text analyzes the relationship between religion and economics, specifically focusing on how Puritan ethics influenced the development of capitalism in northern Europe.

Public housing or subsidized housing projects: housing that is intended for low-income individuals and constructed with funding provided by government agencies. The goal of such constructions is to provide affordable housing, though most housing projects in the United States are challenged by ongoing cycles of poverty.

Racism: social and economic discrimination on the basis of a person's race.

Reflexive: within the social sciences, an approach or interpretation that acknowledges the relationship between cause and effect, with each viewed as affecting the other. This may include readjusting research questions based on trends in data, noting the biases of researchers, and the influence of social or cultural settings.

Rhodes scholarship: an international scholarship at Oxford University given to foreign students to study at Oxford for one year. The scholarship is among the most highly coveted in the world and has been awarded to many students who have gone on to become leading thinkers and scholars in many fields.

Self concept: the awareness and understanding of one's self as an individual, including one's attitudes, beliefs, and opinions.

Social capital: the value of social networks and personal connections from which an individual benefits. An example of positive social capital would be a professional connection that can help secure a job interview.

Social division of labor: the manner in which different kinds of labor (work) are divided according to social class. Upper-class citizens, for example, tend to profit from and control the labor of lower-class citizens.

Social inequality: the unequal distribution of resources and opportunities within a society along the lines of social class. Individuals in higher social classes benefit from more privileges and open access to resources, whereas individuals in the lower class are systematically deprived of access to both.

Social justice: the belief that all individuals in a society deserve equal access to social, economic, and cultural rights, resources and opportunities. Theories of social justice emphasize fairness, justice, and equal rights for all people.

Social reproduction: an idea originally proposed by Karl Marx intended to reveal how social structures are recreated between generations. According to this view, schools play a fundamental role in educating children to occupy their inherited social status in a capitalist society.

Social structure: the system of social networks through which individuals of a group, culture, or society interact with one another.

Socioeconomic: pertaining to the combination of social and economic factors, and concerned with the relationship between the two.

Sociology: the study of the origins, causes, developments, and structure of group, or social, behavior.

Structural-functionalism: a sociological theory in which social structures are understood as being composed of interrelated customs, institutions, and beliefs that function together. In this way, society can be understood to function in a manner analogous to an organism.

Structural inequality: social and economic inequality caused and maintained by social structures (schools, for example).

Structuralism: a theory in the fields of anthropology, sociology, and linguistics in which human behavior, beliefs, and language are best understood by studying the relationship between culture and social structures.

Suburban: the residential suburbs of a city, as opposed to the urban center or rural settlements.

Upward mobility: the ability of members of the lower class to move into the middle or upper class depending on social and economic success.

Vocational training: education that prepares students for jobs in a vocation (a specific area of employment). Students study only those topics most relevant to their intended job.

Welfare: in the United States, federal assistance programs that are intended to provide a minimal level of care and support for poor Americans. Examples include health care, food stamps, unemployment benefits, and assistance with childcare.

Working class: within a capitalist economy, the working classes are the people who are employed in manual (e.g. construction worker), service (e.g. fast food industry), and industrial labor (e.g. equipment operator) jobs.

PEOPLE MENTIONED IN THE TEXT

Pierre Bourdieu (1930–2002) was a French sociologist and anthropologist most well known for his contributions that explained how power relations within society are maintained across generations. MacLeod follows Bourdieu's concepts of capital, concern with social reproduction, and interest in the relationship between social classes.

Samuel Bowles (b.1939) is an American economist who focuses on microeconomic analysis of free-market economies. Bowles is known for investigating themes of selfishness, altruism, and how economic success and inequality are related to one another.

Émile Durkheim (1858–1917) was a French sociologist who helped establish the discipline of sociology in the late nineteenth century. Durkheim focused on the structures of societies and the consequences of these structures for individuals—pioneering practice and theory in the field of sociology and establishing groundwork for generations of later scholars.

Herbert Gintis (b. 1940) is an American economist best known for his study of cooperation, altruistic behavior, and human capital. Gintis works and publishes extensively with Samuel Bowles, with whom he published a landmark study of the role schools play in the social reproduction of American capitalist society.

David Karen is an American sociologist currently focused on the study of the sociology of sports. Karen was a mentor and colleague of MacLeod's and contributed, along with Katherine McClelland, to the analysis of MacLeod's third and final interviews with the Hallway Hangers and the Brothers.

Karl Marx (1818–83) was the nineteenth-century German economist, sociologist, and philosopher known as one of the century's most influential thinkers. Marx developed communist theory and, in doing so, elucidated the exploitative structure of capitalist modes of production.

Katherine McClelland is professor and chair of sociology at Franklin & Marshall College in Pennsylvania. She was a mentor of MacLeod's and helped complete the analysis of the third edition of *Ain't No Makin' It*.

Robert K. Merton (1910–2003) was an American sociologist who is recognized as one of the most influential sociologists of the twentieth century. He is known for establishing the sociological study of science and his search for theories of explanation that would continue to generate new lines of inquiry.

Talcott Parsons (1902–79) was an American sociologist best known for his research on social behavior, social function, and the role that shared social values play in creating stable societies. Parsons contributed greatly to American sociology and the understanding of structural-functionalism in the 1950s.

Ronald Reagan (1911–2004) was the 40th president of the United States, serving two terms from 1981 to 1989. Ronald Reagan had served as the 33rd governor of California (1967–75) and had previously been an actor. Reagan's economic policies, or "Reaganomics," resulted in increased wealth for the wealthy and a then all-time-high gap in wealth between the rich and the poor.

Ferdinand de Saussure (1857–1913) was a Swiss scholar best known for his seminal contributions in the field of linguistics. Saussure argued that the relationships between the parts of languages, not just the parts themselves, were important in understanding how humans construct meaning via language. This approach is the origin of structuralism, which made a considerable impact in the fields of sociology, anthropology, literary criticism, and linguistics.

Max Weber (1864–1920) is best known for his contribution to the sociology of religion and the economy. Weber focused on how religion influenced economies, famously authoring *The Protestant Ethic and the Spirit of Capitalism*, an investigation of the relationship between European Protestant religion and the rise of capitalism in European societies. Together with Karl Marx and Émile Durkheim, Weber is responsible for helping to found sociology.

Paul Willis (b. 1950) is a British sociologist best known for his 1977 study of working-class youth in England. Willis is also known for his focus on the daily life and experience of the middle class, the outstanding quality of his field interviews, and as a founding editor of the journal *Ethnography.*

WORKS CITED

WORKS CITED

Akom, A. A., S. Ginwright, and J. Cammarota. "Youthtopias: Towards a New Paradigm of Critical Youth Studies." *Youth Media Reporter: The Professional Journal of the Youth Media Field* 2, no. 4 (2008). Accessed September 30, 2015. http://iseeed.org/wp-content/uploads/2012/12/Akom_Youthtopias-YMR-Article.pdf.

Bourdieu, Pierre. *Outline of a Theory of Practice.* Cambridge: Cambridge University Press, 1977.

Bowles, Samuel, and Herbert Gintis. *Schooling in Capitalist America.* New York: Basic Books, 1976.

Butts, Jeffrey A., and Jeremy Travis. "The Rise and Fall of American Youth Violence: 1980 to 2000." *Urban Institute* (2002). Accessed September 30, 2105. http://www.urban.org/research/publication/rise-and-fall-american-youth-violence/view/full_report.

Collins, James. "Social Reproduction in Classrooms and Schools." *Annual Review of Anthropology* 38 (2009): 33–48.

Contemporary Sociology. "Books mentioned multiple times on lists of books, which we would like to see in the sociology section of our local bookstores." *Contemporary Sociology* 28 (1999): 159.

Côté, James, and Anton Allahar. "Response to 'Anxious Academics: Mission Drift and Sliding Standards in the Modern Canadian University.'" *Canadian Journal of Sociology* 33, no. 2 (2008): 1069–72.

Demby, Gene. "The Truth Behind the Lies of the Original 'Welfare Queen.'" *National Public Radio.* December 20, 2013. Accessed November 18, 2015. http://www.npr.org/sections/codeswitch/2013/12/20/255819681/the-truth-behind-the-lies-of-the-original-welfare-queen.

Dreier, Peter. "Reagan's Legacy: Homelessness in America." *National Housing Institute* 135 (2004). Accessed September 30, 2015. http://www.nhi.org/online/issues/135/reagan.html.

Espitia, Nicolaus R. "Review of *Ain't No Makin' It: Aspirations and Attainment in a Low-Income Neighborhood* by Jay MacLeod." *Journal of Applied Social Science* 3 (2009): 81–4.

Ferguson, Susan J. "Still No Makin' It: Review of *Ain't No Makin' It: Aspirations and Attainment in a Low-Income Neighborhood* by Jay MacLeod." *Contexts* 8 (2009): 74–6.

Fumanti, Mattia. "Review of 'Representing Youth: Methodological Issues in Critical Youth Studies by Amy L. Best.'" *Journal of the Royal Anthropological Institute* 15, no. 4 (2009): 875–6.

Hochschild, Jennifer L. "Review of *Ain't No Makin' It: Leveled Aspirations in a Low-Income Neighborhood* by Jay MacLeod." *American Journal of Sociology* 94, no. 1 (1988): 182–4.

Kiessling, Roland, and Maarten Mous. "Urban Youth Languages in Africa." *Anthropological Linguistics* 46, no. 3 (2004): 303–41.

MacLeod, Jay. *Ain't No Makin' It: Aspirations and Attainment in a Low-Income Neighborhood.* Boulder, Colorado: Westview Press, 2009.

"Bridging School and Street." *Journal of Negro Education* 60, no. 3 (1991): 260–75.

Minds Stayed on Freedom: The Civil Rights Struggle In the Rural South: An Oral History. Boulder, Colorado: Westview Press, 1991.

Marable, Manning. *Race, Reform, and Rebellion: The Second Reconstruction in Black America 1945–1990.* Jackson: University Press of Mississippi, 1991.

McClelland, Katherine, and David Karen. "Analysis," in *Ain't No Makin' It* by Jay MacLeod, 409–63. Boulder, Colorado: Westview Press, 2009.

Merton, Robert K. *Social Theory and Social Structure.* New York: Free Press, 1968.

National Center for Children in Poverty. "Child Poverty." *National Center for Children in Poverty.* Accessed September 30, 2015. http://www.nccp.org/topics/childpoverty.html.

Newman, Katherine. "Review of *Ain't No Makin' it: Aspirations and Attainments in a Low-Income Neighborhood* by Jay MacLeod." *American Ethnologist* 23, no. 3 (1996): 644–5.

O'Regan, Katherine M., and John M. Quigley. "Where Youth Live: Economic Effects of Urban Space on Employment Prospects." *Urban Studies* 35, no. 7 (1998): 1187–205.

Parsons, Talcott, and Edward A. Shils. *Toward a General Theory of Action.* Cambridge: Harvard University Press, 1976.

Parsons, Talcott, Edward Shils, Kaspar D. Naegele, and Jesse R. Pitts. *Theories of Society: Foundations of Modern Sociological Theory.* New York: Free Press, 1961.

Rao, M. S. A. "Sociology in the 1980s." *Economic and Political Weekly* 14, no. 44 (1979): 1810–15.

Roberts, Steven V. "Reagan on Homelessness: Many Choose to Live in the Streets." *New York Times,* December 23, 1988. Accessed November 18, 2015. http://www.nytimes.com/1988/12/23/us/reagan-on-homelessness-many-choose-to-live-in-the-streets.html.

Royster, Deirdre. "Review of *Ain't No Makin It: Aspirations and Attainment in a Low-Income Neighborhood* by Jay MacLeod." *Contemporary Sociology* 25, no. 2 (1996): 151–3.

Sennett, Richard, and Jonathan Cobb. *The Hidden Injuries of Class.* New York: Vintage Books, 1972.

Spaaij, Ramón, Jonathan Magee, and Ruth Jeanes. "Urban Youth, Worklessness and Sport: A Comparison of Sports-based Employability Programmes in Rotterdam and Stoke-on Trent." *Urban Studies* 50, no. 8 (2013): 1608–24.

The State of Working America. "Poverty." *The State of Working America.* Accessed September 30, 2015. http://stateofworkingamerica.org/fact-sheets/poverty/.

West, Cornell. *Race Matters.* Boston: Beacon Press, 1993.

Young, Alford A., Jr. "Review of *Ain't No Makin' It: Aspirations and Attainment in a Low-Income Neighborhood* by Jay McLeod." *American Journal of Sociology* 101, no. 6 (1996): 1758–60.

THE MACAT LIBRARY BY DISCIPLINE

AFRICANA STUDIES

Chinua Achebe's *An Image of Africa: Racism in Conrad's Heart of Darkness*
W. E. B. Du Bois's *The Souls of Black Folk*
Zora Neale Huston's *Characteristics of Negro Expression*
Martin Luther King Jr's *Why We Can't Wait*
Toni Morrison's *Playing in the Dark: Whiteness in the American Literary Imagination*

ANTHROPOLOGY

Arjun Appadurai's *Modernity at Large: Cultural Dimensions of Globalisation*
Philippe Ariès's *Centuries of Childhood*
Franz Boas's *Race, Language and Culture*
Kim Chan & Renée Mauborgne's *Blue Ocean Strategy*
Jared Diamond's *Guns, Germs & Steel: the Fate of Human Societies*
Jared Diamond's *Collapse: How Societies Choose to Fail or Survive*
E. E. Evans-Pritchard's *Witchcraft, Oracles and Magic Among the Azande*
James Ferguson's *The Anti-Politics Machine*
Clifford Geertz's *The Interpretation of Cultures*
David Graeber's *Debt: the First 5000 Years*
Karen Ho's *Liquidated: An Ethnography of Wall Street*
Geert Hofstede's *Culture's Consequences: Comparing Values, Behaviors, Institutes and Organizations across Nations*
Claude Lévi-Strauss's *Structural Anthropology*
Jay Macleod's *Ain't No Makin' It: Aspirations and Attainment in a Low-Income Neighborhood*
Saba Mahmood's *The Politics of Piety: The Islamic Revival and the Feminist Subject*
Marcel Mauss's *The Gift*

BUSINESS

Jean Lave & Etienne Wenger's *Situated Learning*
Theodore Levitt's *Marketing Myopia*
Burton G. Malkiel's *A Random Walk Down Wall Street*
Douglas McGregor's *The Human Side of Enterprise*
Michael Porter's *Competitive Strategy: Creating and Sustaining Superior Performance*
John Kotter's *Leading Change*
C. K. Prahalad & Gary Hamel's *The Core Competence of the Corporation*

CRIMINOLOGY

Michelle Alexander's *The New Jim Crow: Mass Incarceration in the Age of Colorblindness*
Michael R. Gottfredson & Travis Hirschi's *A General Theory of Crime*
Richard Herrnstein & Charles A. Murray's *The Bell Curve: Intelligence and Class Structure in American Life*
Elizabeth Loftus's *Eyewitness Testimony*
Jay Macleod's *Ain't No Makin' It: Aspirations and Attainment in a Low-Income Neighborhood*
Philip Zimbardo's *The Lucifer Effect*

ECONOMICS

Janet Abu-Lughod's *Before European Hegemony*
Ha-Joon Chang's *Kicking Away the Ladder*
David Brion Davis's *The Problem of Slavery in the Age of Revolution*
Milton Friedman's *The Role of Monetary Policy*
Milton Friedman's *Capitalism and Freedom*
David Graeber's *Debt: the First 5000 Years*
Friedrich Hayek's *The Road to Serfdom*
Karen Ho's *Liquidated: An Ethnography of Wall Street*

John Maynard Keynes's *The General Theory of Employment, Interest and Money*
Charles P. Kindleberger's *Manias, Panics and Crashes*
Robert Lucas's *Why Doesn't Capital Flow from Rich to Poor Countries?*
Burton G. Malkiel's *A Random Walk Down Wall Street*
Thomas Robert Malthus's *An Essay on the Principle of Population*
Karl Marx's *Capital*
Thomas Piketty's *Capital in the Twenty-First Century*
Amartya Sen's *Development as Freedom*
Adam Smith's *The Wealth of Nations*
Nassim Nicholas Taleb's *The Black Swan: The Impact of the Highly Improbable*
Amos Tversky's & Daniel Kahneman's *Judgment under Uncertainty: Heuristics and Biases*
Mahbub Ul Haq's *Reflections on Human Development*
Max Weber's *The Protestant Ethic and the Spirit of Capitalism*

FEMINISM AND GENDER STUDIES

Judith Butler's *Gender Trouble*
Simone De Beauvoir's *The Second Sex*
Michel Foucault's *History of Sexuality*
Betty Friedan's *The Feminine Mystique*
Saba Mahmood's *The Politics of Piety: The Islamic Revival and the Feminist Subject*
Joan Wallach Scott's *Gender and the Politics of History*
Mary Wollstonecraft's *A Vindication of the Rights of Women*
Virginia Woolf's *A Room of One's Own*

GEOGRAPHY

The Brundtland Report's *Our Common Future*
Rachel Carson's *Silent Spring*
Charles Darwin's *On the Origin of Species*
James Ferguson's *The Anti-Politics Machine*
Jane Jacobs's *The Death and Life of Great American Cities*
James Lovelock's *Gaia: A New Look at Life on Earth*
Amartya Sen's *Development as Freedom*
Mathis Wackernagel & William Rees's *Our Ecological Footprint*

HISTORY

Janet Abu-Lughod's *Before European Hegemony*
Benedict Anderson's *Imagined Communities*
Bernard Bailyn's *The Ideological Origins of the American Revolution*
Hanna Batatu's *The Old Social Classes And The Revolutionary Movements Of Iraq*
Christopher Browning's *Ordinary Men: Reserve Police Batallion 101 and the Final Solution in Poland*
Edmund Burke's *Reflections on the Revolution in France*
William Cronon's *Nature's Metropolis: Chicago And The Great West*
Alfred W. Crosby's *The Columbian Exchange*
Hamid Dabashi's *Iran: A People Interrupted*
David Brion Davis's *The Problem of Slavery in the Age of Revolution*
Nathalie Zemon Davis's *The Return of Martin Guerre*
Jared Diamond's *Guns, Germs & Steel: the Fate of Human Societies*
Frank Dikotter's *Mao's Great Famine*
John W Dower's *War Without Mercy: Race And Power In The Pacific War*
W. E. B. Du Bois's *The Souls of Black Folk*
Richard J. Evans's *In Defence of History*
Lucien Febvre's *The Problem of Unbelief in the 16th Century*
Sheila Fitzpatrick's *Everyday Stalinism*

Eric Foner's *Reconstruction: America's Unfinished Revolution, 1863-1877*
Michel Foucault's *Discipline and Punish*
Michel Foucault's *History of Sexuality*
Francis Fukuyama's *The End of History and the Last Man*
John Lewis Gaddis's *We Now Know: Rethinking Cold War History*
Ernest Gellner's *Nations and Nationalism*
Eugene Genovese's *Roll, Jordan, Roll: The World the Slaves Made*
Carlo Ginzburg's *The Night Battles*
Daniel Goldhagen's *Hitler's Willing Executioners*
Jack Goldstone's *Revolution and Rebellion in the Early Modern World*
Antonio Gramsci's *The Prison Notebooks*
Alexander Hamilton, John Jay & James Madison's *The Federalist Papers*
Christopher Hill's *The World Turned Upside Down*
Carole Hillenbrand's *The Crusades: Islamic Perspectives*
Thomas Hobbes's *Leviathan*
Eric Hobsbawm's *The Age Of Revolution*
John A. Hobson's *Imperialism: A Study*
Albert Hourani's *History of the Arab Peoples*
Samuel P. Huntington's *The Clash of Civilizations and the Remaking of World Order*
C. L. R. James's *The Black Jacobins*
Tony Judt's *Postwar: A History of Europe Since 1945*
Ernst Kantorowicz's *The King's Two Bodies: A Study in Medieval Political Theology*
Paul Kennedy's *The Rise and Fall of the Great Powers*
Ian Kershaw's *The "Hitler Myth": Image and Reality in the Third Reich*
John Maynard Keynes's *The General Theory of Employment, Interest and Money*
Charles P. Kindleberger's *Manias, Panics and Crashes*
Martin Luther King Jr's *Why We Can't Wait*
Henry Kissinger's *World Order: Reflections on the Character of Nations and the Course of History*
Thomas Kuhn's *The Structure of Scientific Revolutions*
Georges Lefebvre's *The Coming of the French Revolution*
John Locke's *Two Treatises of Government*
Niccolò Machiavelli's *The Prince*
Thomas Robert Malthus's *An Essay on the Principle of Population*
Mahmood Mamdani's *Citizen and Subject: Contemporary Africa And The Legacy Of Late Colonialism*
Karl Marx's *Capital*
Stanley Milgram's *Obedience to Authority*
John Stuart Mill's *On Liberty*
Thomas Paine's *Common Sense*
Thomas Paine's *Rights of Man*
Geoffrey Parker's *Global Crisis: War, Climate Change and Catastrophe in the Seventeenth Century*
Jonathan Riley-Smith's *The First Crusade and the Idea of Crusading*
Jean-Jacques Rousseau's *The Social Contract*
Joan Wallach Scott's *Gender and the Politics of History*
Theda Skocpol's *States and Social Revolutions*
Adam Smith's *The Wealth of Nations*
Timothy Snyder's *Bloodlands: Europe Between Hitler and Stalin*
Sun Tzu's *The Art of War*
Keith Thomas's *Religion and the Decline of Magic*
Thucydides's *The History of the Peloponnesian War*
Frederick Jackson Turner's *The Significance of the Frontier in American History*
Odd Arne Westad's *The Global Cold War: Third World Interventions And The Making Of Our Times*

LITERATURE

Chinua Achebe's *An Image of Africa: Racism in Conrad's Heart of Darkness*
Roland Barthes's *Mythologies*
Homi K. Bhabha's *The Location of Culture*
Judith Butler's *Gender Trouble*
Simone De Beauvoir's *The Second Sex*
Ferdinand De Saussure's *Course in General Linguistics*
T. S. Eliot's *The Sacred Wood: Essays on Poetry and Criticism*
Zora Neale Huston's *Characteristics of Negro Expression*
Toni Morrison's *Playing in the Dark: Whiteness in the American Literary Imagination*
Edward Said's *Orientalism*
Gayatri Chakravorty Spivak's *Can the Subaltern Speak?*
Mary Wollstonecraft's *A Vindication of the Rights of Women*
Virginia Woolf's *A Room of One's Own*

PHILOSOPHY

Elizabeth Anscombe's *Modern Moral Philosophy*
Hannah Arendt's *The Human Condition*
Aristotle's *Metaphysics*
Aristotle's *Nicomachean Ethics*
Edmund Gettier's *Is Justified True Belief Knowledge?*
Georg Wilhelm Friedrich Hegel's *Phenomenology of Spirit*
David Hume's *Dialogues Concerning Natural Religion*
David Hume's *The Enquiry for Human Understanding*
Immanuel Kant's *Religion within the Boundaries of Mere Reason*
Immanuel Kant's *Critique of Pure Reason*
Søren Kierkegaard's *The Sickness Unto Death*
Søren Kierkegaard's *Fear and Trembling*
C. S. Lewis's *The Abolition of Man*
Alasdair MacIntyre's *After Virtue*
Marcus Aurelius's *Meditations*
Friedrich Nietzsche's *On the Genealogy of Morality*
Friedrich Nietzsche's *Beyond Good and Evil*
Plato's *Republic*
Plato's *Symposium*
Jean-Jacques Rousseau's *The Social Contract*
Gilbert Ryle's *The Concept of Mind*
Baruch Spinoza's *Ethics*
Sun Tzu's *The Art of War*
Ludwig Wittgenstein's *Philosophical Investigations*

POLITICS

Benedict Anderson's *Imagined Communities*
Aristotle's *Politics*
Bernard Bailyn's *The Ideological Origins of the American Revolution*
Edmund Burke's *Reflections on the Revolution in France*
John C. Calhoun's *A Disquisition on Government*
Ha-Joon Chang's *Kicking Away the Ladder*
Hamid Dabashi's *Iran: A People Interrupted*
Hamid Dabashi's *Theology of Discontent: The Ideological Foundation of the Islamic Revolution in Iran*
Robert Dahl's *Democracy and its Critics*
Robert Dahl's *Who Governs?*
David Brion Davis's *The Problem of Slavery in the Age of Revolution*

Alexis De Tocqueville's *Democracy in America*
James Ferguson's *The Anti-Politics Machine*
Frank Dikotter's *Mao's Great Famine*
Sheila Fitzpatrick's *Everyday Stalinism*
Eric Foner's *Reconstruction: America's Unfinished Revolution, 1863-1877*
Milton Friedman's *Capitalism and Freedom*
Francis Fukuyama's *The End of History and the Last Man*
John Lewis Gaddis's *We Now Know: Rethinking Cold War History*
Ernest Gellner's *Nations and Nationalism*
David Graeber's *Debt: the First 5000 Years*
Antonio Gramsci's *The Prison Notebooks*
Alexander Hamilton, John Jay & James Madison's *The Federalist Papers*
Friedrich Hayek's *The Road to Serfdom*
Christopher Hill's *The World Turned Upside Down*
Thomas Hobbes's *Leviathan*
John A. Hobson's *Imperialism: A Study*
Samuel P. Huntington's *The Clash of Civilizations and the Remaking of World Order*
Tony Judt's *Postwar: A History of Europe Since 1945*
David C. Kang's *China Rising: Peace, Power and Order in East Asia*
Paul Kennedy's *The Rise and Fall of Great Powers*
Robert Keohane's *After Hegemony*
Martin Luther King Jr.'s *Why We Can't Wait*
Henry Kissinger's *World Order: Reflections on the Character of Nations and the Course of History*
John Locke's *Two Treatises of Government*
Niccolò Machiavelli's *The Prince*
Thomas Robert Malthus's *An Essay on the Principle of Population*
Mahmood Mamdani's *Citizen and Subject: Contemporary Africa And The Legacy Of Late Colonialism*
Karl Marx's *Capital*
John Stuart Mill's *On Liberty*
John Stuart Mill's *Utilitarianism*
Hans Morgenthau's *Politics Among Nations*
Thomas Paine's *Common Sense*
Thomas Paine's *Rights of Man*
Thomas Piketty's *Capital in the Twenty-First Century*
Robert D. Putman's *Bowling Alone*
John Rawls's *Theory of Justice*
Jean-Jacques Rousseau's *The Social Contract*
Theda Skocpol's *States and Social Revolutions*
Adam Smith's *The Wealth of Nations*
Sun Tzu's *The Art of War*
Henry David Thoreau's *Civil Disobedience*
Thucydides's *The History of the Peloponnesian War*
Kenneth Waltz's *Theory of International Politics*
Max Weber's *Politics as a Vocation*
Odd Arne Westad's *The Global Cold War: Third World Interventions And The Making Of Our Times*

POSTCOLONIAL STUDIES

Roland Barthes's *Mythologies*
Frantz Fanon's *Black Skin, White Masks*
Homi K. Bhabha's *The Location of Culture*
Gustavo Gutiérrez's *A Theology of Liberation*
Edward Said's *Orientalism*
Gayatri Chakravorty Spivak's *Can the Subaltern Speak?*

PSYCHOLOGY

Gordon Allport's *The Nature of Prejudice*
Alan Baddeley & Graham Hitch's *Aggression: A Social Learning Analysis*
Albert Bandura's *Aggression: A Social Learning Analysis*
Leon Festinger's *A Theory of Cognitive Dissonance*
Sigmund Freud's *The Interpretation of Dreams*
Betty Friedan's *The Feminine Mystique*
Michael R. Gottfredson & Travis Hirschi's *A General Theory of Crime*
Eric Hoffer's *The True Believer: Thoughts on the Nature of Mass Movements*
William James's *Principles of Psychology*
Elizabeth Loftus's *Eyewitness Testimony*
A. H. Maslow's *A Theory of Human Motivation*
Stanley Milgram's *Obedience to Authority*
Steven Pinker's *The Better Angels of Our Nature*
Oliver Sacks's *The Man Who Mistook His Wife For a Hat*
Richard Thaler & Cass Sunstein's *Nudge: Improving Decisions About Health, Wealth and Happiness*
Amos Tversky's *Judgment under Uncertainty: Heuristics and Biases*
Philip Zimbardo's *The Lucifer Effect*

SCIENCE

Rachel Carson's *Silent Spring*
William Cronon's *Nature's Metropolis: Chicago And The Great West*
Alfred W. Crosby's *The Columbian Exchange*
Charles Darwin's *On the Origin of Species*
Richard Dawkin's *The Selfish Gene*
Thomas Kuhn's *The Structure of Scientific Revolutions*
Geoffrey Parker's *Global Crisis: War, Climate Change and Catastrophe in the Seventeenth Century*
Mathis Wackernagel & William Rees's *Our Ecological Footprint*

SOCIOLOGY

Michelle Alexander's *The New Jim Crow: Mass Incarceration in the Age of Colorblindness*
Gordon Allport's *The Nature of Prejudice*
Albert Bandura's *Aggression: A Social Learning Analysis*
Hanna Batatu's *The Old Social Classes And The Revolutionary Movements Of Iraq*
Ha-Joon Chang's *Kicking Away the Ladder*
W. E. B. Du Bois's *The Souls of Black Folk*
Émile Durkheim's *On Suicide*
Frantz Fanon's *Black Skin, White Masks*
Frantz Fanon's *The Wretched of the Earth*
Eric Foner's *Reconstruction: America's Unfinished Revolution, 1863-1877*
Eugene Genovese's *Roll, Jordan, Roll: The World the Slaves Made*
Jack Goldstone's *Revolution and Rebellion in the Early Modern World*
Antonio Gramsci's *The Prison Notebooks*
Richard Herrnstein & Charles A Murray's *The Bell Curve: Intelligence and Class Structure in American Life*
Eric Hoffer's *The True Believer: Thoughts on the Nature of Mass Movements*
Jane Jacobs's *The Death and Life of Great American Cities*
Robert Lucas's *Why Doesn't Capital Flow from Rich to Poor Countries?*
Jay Macleod's *Ain't No Makin' It: Aspirations and Attainment in a Low Income Neighborhood*
Elaine May's *Homeward Bound: American Families in the Cold War Era*
Douglas McGregor's *The Human Side of Enterprise*
C. Wright Mills's *The Sociological Imagination*

Thomas Piketty's *Capital in the Twenty-First Century*
Robert D. Putman's *Bowling Alone*
David Riesman's *The Lonely Crowd: A Study of the Changing American Character*
Edward Said's *Orientalism*
Joan Wallach Scott's *Gender and the Politics of History*
Theda Skocpol's *States and Social Revolutions*
Max Weber's *The Protestant Ethic and the Spirit of Capitalism*

THEOLOGY

Augustine's *Confessions*
Benedict's *Rule of St Benedict*
Gustavo Gutiérrez's *A Theology of Liberation*
Carole Hillenbrand's *The Crusades: Islamic Perspectives*
David Hume's *Dialogues Concerning Natural Religion*
Immanuel Kant's *Religion within the Boundaries of Mere Reason*
Ernst Kantorowicz's *The King's Two Bodies: A Study in Medieval Political Theology*
Søren Kierkegaard's *The Sickness Unto Death*
C. S. Lewis's *The Abolition of Man*
Saba Mahmood's *The Politics of Piety: The Islamic Revival and the Feminist Subject*
Baruch Spinoza's *Ethics*
Keith Thomas's *Religion and the Decline of Magic*

COMING SOON

Chris Argyris's *The Individual and the Organisation*
Seyla Benhabib's *The Rights of Others*
Walter Benjamin's *The Work Of Art in the Age of Mechanical Reproduction*
John Berger's *Ways of Seeing*
Pierre Bourdieu's *Outline of a Theory of Practice*
Mary Douglas's *Purity and Danger*
Roland Dworkin's *Taking Rights Seriously*
James G. March's *Exploration and Exploitation in Organisational Learning*
Ikujiro Nonaka's *A Dynamic Theory of Organizational Knowledge Creation*
Griselda Pollock's *Vision and Difference*
Amartya Sen's *Inequality Re-Examined*
Susan Sontag's *On Photography*
Yasser Tabbaa's *The Transformation of Islamic Art*
Ludwig von Mises's *Theory of Money and Credit*

Macat Pairs

Analyse historical and modern issues from opposite sides of an argument. Pairs include:

HOW TO RUN AN ECONOMY

John Maynard Keynes's

The General Theory OF Employment, Interest and Money

Classical economics suggests that market economies are self-correcting in times of recession or depression, and tend toward full employment and output. But English economist John Maynard Keynes disagrees.

In his ground-breaking 1936 study *The General Theory*, Keynes argues that traditional economics has misunderstood the causes of unemployment. Employment is not determined by the price of labor; it is directly linked to demand. Keynes believes market economies are by nature unstable, and so require government intervention. Spurred on by the social catastrophe of the Great Depression of the 1930s, he sets out to revolutionize the way the world thinks

Milton Friedman's

The Role of Monetary Policy

Friedman's 1968 paper changed the course of economic theory. In just 17 pages, he demolished existing theory and outlined an effective alternate monetary policy designed to secure 'high employment, stable prices and rapid growth.'

Friedman demonstrated that monetary policy plays a vital role in broader economic stability and argued that economists got their monetary policy wrong in the 1950s and 1960s by misunderstanding the relationship between inflation and unemployment. Previous generations of economists had believed that governments could permanently decrease unemployment by permitting inflation—and vice versa. Friedman's most original contribution was to show that this supposed trade-off is an illusion that only works in the short term.

Macat analyses are available from all good bookshops and libraries.

Access hundreds of analyses through one, multimedia tool.
Join free for one month **library.macat.com**

Macat Pairs

Analyse historical and modern issues from opposite sides of an argument. Pairs include:

ARE WE FUNDAMENTALLY GOOD - OR BAD?

Steven Pinker's

The Better Angels of Our Nature

Stephen Pinker's gloriously optimistic 2011 book argues that, despite humanity's biological tendency toward violence, we are, in fact, less violent today than ever before. To prove his case, Pinker lays out pages of detailed statistical evidence. For him, much of the credit for the decline goes to the eighteenth-century Enlightenment movement, whose ideas of liberty, tolerance, and respect for the value of human life filtered down through society and affected how people thought. That psychological change led to behavioral change—and overall we became more peaceful. Critics countered that humanity could never overcome the biological urge toward violence; others argued that Pinker's statistics were flawed.

Philip Zimbardo's

The Lucifer Effect

Some psychologists believe those who commit cruelty are innately evil. Zimbardo disagrees. In *The Lucifer Effect*, he argues that sometimes good people do evil things simply because of the situations they find themselves in, citing many historical examples to illustrate his point. Zimbardo details his 1971 Stanford prison experiment, where ordinary volunteers playing guards in a mock prison rapidly became abusive. But he also describes the tortures committed by US army personnel in Iraq's Abu Ghraib prison in 2003—and how he himself testified in defence of one of those guards. committed by US army personnel in Iraq's Abu Ghraib prison in 2003—and how he himself testified in defence of one of those guards.

Macat analyses are available from all good bookshops and libraries.

Access hundreds of analyses through one, multimedia tool.
Join free for one month **library.macat.com**

Macat Pairs

Analyse historical and modern issues from opposite sides of an argument. Pairs include:

HOW WE RELATE TO EACH OTHER AND SOCIETY

Jean-Jacques Rousseau's
The Social Contract

Rousseau's famous work sets out the radical concept of the 'social contract': a give-and-take relationship between individual freedom and social order.

If people are free to do as they like, governed only by their own sense of justice, they are also vulnerable to chaos and violence. To avoid this, Rousseau proposes, they should agree to give up some freedom to benefit from the protection of social and political organization. But this deal is only just if societies are led by the collective needs and desires of the people, and able to control the private interests of individuals. For Rousseau, the only legitimate form of government is rule by the people.

Robert D. Putnam's
Bowling Alone

In *Bowling Alone*, Robert Putnam argues that Americans have become disconnected from one another and from the institutions of their common life, and investigates the consequences of this change.

Looking at a range of indicators, from membership in formal organizations to the number of invitations being extended to informal dinner parties, Putnam demonstrates that Americans are interacting less and creating less "social capital" – with potentially disastrous implications for their society.

It would be difficult to overstate the impact of *Bowling Alone*, one of the most frequently cited social science publications of the last half-century.

Macat analyses are available from all good bookshops and libraries.

Access hundreds of analyses through one, multimedia tool.
Join free for one month **library.macat.com**

Printed in the United States
by Baker & Taylor Publisher Services